[The Buddha] gave myriad teachings designed to suit our diverse interests and dispositions. . . . The extensive and profound scriptures containing those teachings, called sutras, outline the methods and means to bring happiness to all beings. . . . In Tibet, the Buddhist teachings were compiled to reveal the stages of the entire path to enlightenment in a single book. . . . I do not claim to have great knowledge or high realization, but remembering the kindness of my teachers, who gave these instructions to me, and with concern for the welfare of all beings, I offer these teachings to you."

—*from the Introduction*

So begins *The Way to Freedom*, the Dalai Lama's gentle and profoundly eloquent exposition of the Buddha's teachings and instructions. With unprecedented simplicity and beauty, the Dalai Lama reveals the essence of Tibetan Buddhism to both newcomers and devotees. He discusses the tumultuous history

(continued on back flap)

The Way to Freedom

The Path to Enlightenment Series

THE WAY TO FREEDOM

THE LIBRARY OF TIBET

THE WAY TO
FREEDOM

by

His Holiness,
The Dalai Lama of Tibet

GENERAL SERIES EDITOR, JOHN F. AVEDON

EDITOR, DONALD S. LOPEZ, JR.

HarperSanFrancisco
A Division of HarperCollins*Publishers*

Book design by David Bullen

FIRST EDITION

Library of Congress Cataloging-in-Publication Data

Bstan-'dzin-ryga-mtsho, Dalai Lama XIV.
The way to freedom / Dalai Lama :
edited by Donald S. Lopez, Jr. — 1st ed.
p. cm — (The Library of Tibet)
ISBN 0–06–061722–5 (cloth : alk. paper)
1. Buddhism—Doctrines.
I. Lopez, Donald S.   II. Series.
BQ7935.B774W39   1994   94–31891
294.3'42—dc20   CIP

---

95 96 97 ❖   HAD   10 9 8 7 6 5 4 3

CONTENTS

The Way to Freedom

INTRODUCTION

To practice Buddhism is to wage a struggle between the negative and positive forces in your mind. The meditator seeks to

undermine the negative and develop and increase the positive. The teachings in this book are meant to transform the mind; to read or listen to a single passage can bring great benefit.

There are no physical markers by which to measure progress in the struggle between the positive and negative forces in consciousness. Changes begin when you first identify and recognize your delusions, such as anger and jealousy. One then needs to know the antidotes to delusion, and that knowledge is gained by listening to the teachings. There is no simple way to remove delusions. They cannot be extracted surgically. They have to be recognized, and then, through the practice of these teachings, they can be gradually reduced and then completely eliminated.

These teachings offer the means to free oneself from delusion—a path that eventually leads to freedom from all suffering and to the bliss of enlightenment.

The more one comes to understand the Dharma, or Buddhist teachings, the weaker will be the grip of pride, hatred, greed, and other negative emotions that cause so much suffering. Applying this understanding in daily life over a period of months and years will gradually transform the mind, because, despite the fact that it often seems otherwise, the mind is subject to change. If you can compare your state of mind now to your state of mind after you have read this book, you may notice some improvement. If so, these teachings will have served their purpose.

In the present eon, the Buddha appeared over 2,500 years ago in the form of Shakyamuni, the sage of the Shakya clan. He took ordination as a monk and engaged in arduous yogic practices. Seated in meditation under a tree in a place called Bodh Gaya in northern India, he achieved complete enlightenment. Subsequently, he gave myriad teachings designed to suit our diverse interests and dispositions. Some he taught how to gain a better rebirth and others how to gain liberation from the cycle of birth and death. The extensive and profound scriptures containing those teachings, called sutras, outline the methods and means to bring happiness to all beings. Derived from the Buddha's experience and logically sound, these teachings can be practiced and tested by anyone.

In Tibet, the Buddhist teachings were compiled to reveal the stages of the entire path to enlightenment in a single book. In the past, many people have been able to achieve the state of complete enlightenment by relying on these same instructions; they are suited to anyone with an untamed mind. Though we realize the harm caused by our delusions, such as the damage done to ourselves and others when we act out of anger, we still fall under their influence. Thus an untamed mind throws us recklessly into the abyss instead of stopping when it sees the edge.

We have been propelled into this cycle of suffering by our delusions and the actions they provoke, which are known as karma. Because of the cause-and-effect relation between our actions and our experience, we spend our lives enduring all sorts of ups and downs, in trouble and confusion. To be totally free from the weight of past deeds and from the thralldom of desire, hatred, and ignorance is called liberation, or nirvana. When we are able to eliminate delusions and karma by realizing the natural purity of the mind, total peace follows and we gain complete freedom from the cycle of suffering.

If we can do good deeds, such as saving the lives of animals under threat of death, we can accumulate the conditions necessary for gaining rebirth as a human being. If we undertake the serious practice of the Dharma, we will be able to continue our spiritual progress in our lives to come. But this life is precious and unpredictable, and it is important to engage in practice while we have the opportunity. We never know how long that opportunity will last.

What we do now, according to the law of karma, the principle of cause and effect, has consequences for the future. Our future is determined by our present state of mind, but our present state of mind is overrun by delusions. We should aspire to achieve enlightenment. If that is not possible, we should seek to gain freedom from rebirth. If that is not possible, we should at least plant the seeds for a favorable rebirth in the next life, without falling into lower realms of existence. At this auspicious juncture, when we are free of obstacles to hearing and practicing the Dharma, we must not let this rare opportunity pass.

However, freeing ourselves from suffering is only part of the quest. Just as you do not want even the slightest suffering and want only happiness, so also does everyone else. All beings are equal in the sense that all have a natural tendency to wish for happiness and freedom from suffering. All beings have the same right to happiness and freedom from suffering. Knowing this and still working only for our own liberation makes the accomplishment a small one. But if our underlying motivation is to be able to help others, we can attain the omniscient state and with it the capacity to benefit every living being. We can become Buddhas ourselves.

If our present state of mind is poor and our capacity limited, how can we fulfill the wishes of others? The mere wish to help them is not enough. First we must achieve the ability to perceive the diverse aspirations of others. In order for our perception to be clear, we must eliminate all the faults that prevent us from seeing things as they are. The obstacles to omniscience are the imprints left by such delusions as desire, anger, pride, and ignorance. Even after delusions have been eliminated, the mind retains their imprints. But because the true nature of the mind is clear, pure, and knowing, it is possible to purify the mind thoroughly and so attain that clarity of awareness known as omniscience.

The principal motive impelling the Buddha to achieve all his great qualities of body, speech, and mind was compassion. The essence of our practice too should be the wish to help others. Such an altruistic wish is naturally present within our hearts in the acknowledgment that others are just like us in wishing to be happy and to avoid suffering. It is like a seed, which we can protect and help to grow through practice. All the teachings of the Buddha essentially try to develop this kind heart and altruistic mind. The Buddha's path is founded on compassion, the wish that others be free from suffering. This leads us to the understanding that the welfare of others is ultimately more important than our own, for without others, we would have no spiritual practice, no opportunity for enlightenment. I do not claim to have great knowledge or high realization, but remembering the kindness of my teachers, who gave these instructions to me, and with concern for the welfare of all beings, I offer these teachings to you.

CHAPTER I

THE TEACHING

The Buddha arose from meditation 2,500 years ago after attaining enlightenment. The subject of his first teaching was the Four

Noble Truths. The First Noble Truth was the truth of suffering, the fact that our happiness is constantly passing away. Everything we have is subject to impermanence. Nothing within what we commonly think of as real is permanent. Ignorance, attachment, and anger are the causes of our relentless suffering. Thus the Second Noble Truth is to understand this cause of suffering. When you eliminate the root of suffering (the delusions), you achieve a state of the cessation of suffering—the Third Noble Truth, or nirvana. The Fourth Noble Truth is that there exists a path leading to the cessation of suffering. In order to achieve that state within your own mind, you must follow a path.

It is not until we understand the law of karma, or cause and effect, that we are inspired to embark on the path to end suffering. Negative thoughts and actions produce negative results and conditions, just as positive thoughts and actions produce positive results and conditions. When we develop deep conviction in the law of cause and effect, we will be able to perceive the causes and conditions of our own sufferings. Our present happiness or unhappiness is nothing more or less than the result of previous actions. The sufferings themselves are so obvious that our experience testifies to their existence. We will therefore develop the realization that if we do not desire suffering, then we should work to uproot its causes now. Through understanding suffering and its origins we can perceive the possibility of eliminating ignorance, which is the root cause of suffering, and we can conceive of a state of cessation, a total cessation of this ignorance and the delusions induced by it. When our understanding of cessation is perfect, we will develop a strong and spontaneous desire to reach such a state. Our understanding should be so profound that it shakes our whole being and induces in us a spontaneous wish to gain it. Once we develop this spontaneous wish to achieve cessation, an immense appreciation for the beings who have realized this cessation within their own minds develops. The recognition of the Buddha's accomplishments becomes powerful. The benefits and beauty of his teachings become clear.

This teaching of the stages of the path to enlightenment came to Tibet from India. Buddhism did not come to Tibet until the eighth century, but in the ninth century its practice was outlawed by King

Lang-dar-ma. He closed the monasteries, which had been the primary center for teachings, as the Chinese have done today. Lang-dar-ma's destruction of Buddhism was extensive, but it was still possible to practice in remote regions, and the tradition was preserved. In the eleventh century, confusion arose over the existence of two approaches to the practice of the teachings. There was *sutra,* or the path of study and practice by which it takes many lifetimes to achieve enlightenment, and *tantra,* the secret practices by which enlightenment can be achieved even in one lifetime. In the eleventh century, an Indian monk named Atisha became famous for his ability to explain the Buddha's teachings and to defend them in debates with non-Buddhist philosophers. He was able to bring together all the diverse Buddhist philosophical positions that had developed over the centuries as well as the lay and monastic systems of practice. He was regarded as a nonpartisan and authoritative master by all the philosophical schools.

At that time the king of western Tibet, inspired by the great Buddhist faith of his ancestors, read many texts and found what he thought were contradictions among the different systems, especially regarding sutra and tantra. Many Tibetans at that time, due to a misunderstanding of the role of ethics in the two systems, thought that the practices of sutra and tantra could not be undertaken by one person. Yet the king was aware that when Buddhism had arrived in Tibet in the eighth century, the two systems had coexisted peacefully. The

Indian master Shantarakshita had spread both the practice of monastic discipline and the vast and compassionate practices of sutra. At the same time the great yogi, Padmasambhava, was spreading the practices of tantra and taming the malevolent forces that plagued Tibet. These two masters undertook the practices of the Dharma together, without any hostility between them. Realizing that India was the source of the practice of sutra and tantra, the king sent twenty intelligent students from Tibet to study in India with the idea that they would return and clarify the teachings for Tibetans. Many of them died on the way, but two returned and reported to the king that in India the practice of sutra and tantra was undertaken without any difficulties between them. They found the great master, Atisha, at the monastery of Vikramashila in Bengal. Atisha, these students felt, was the one who could help Tibet.

The king himself went in search of enough gold to meet the expenses of inviting this master from India, but he was captured by a king who was hostile to Buddhism. He was given the choice between his life and his search for the Dharma. When he refused to give up his search, he was imprisoned. His nephew tried to rescue him, but the king said, "You should not bother about me. Do not waste a single gold coin on my ransom. Use all the gold to invite Atisha from India." The nephew did not obey his uncle and eventually offered the king's weight in gold as ransom. But the kidnapper refused it, saying the nephew had brought gold equal only to the weight of his uncle's body, but not enough for his head. He refused to release the prisoner until he had brought more gold. The nephew then told his uncle what had happened. "If I wage a war to rescue you," the nephew explained, "there will be great bloodshed. So I will try to collect the gold for your head. Please pray that I will be successful." His uncle replied, "It is my wish to bring the light of the Dharma to Tibet to clarify all doubts and contradictions. If my wish is fulfilled, even if I have to die here, I will have no regrets. I am an old man; sooner or later I will have to die. I have taken rebirth over many lifetimes, but it is very rare that I have been able to sacrifice my life for the sake of the Dharma. Today I have been granted that opportunity. So send word to Atisha himself telling him that I have given up my life so that he could be invited to Tibet and that my last wish is that he come to Tibet and spread the message of the Buddha and clarify our misunderstandings." Hearing his uncle's determination, the nephew was greatly moved. With tremendous sadness he bade his uncle farewell.

The nephew sent a group of Tibetan translators to India in search of Atisha. The six companions, taking seven hundred gold coins, eventually arrived at Atisha's monastery, where they were taken to see the abbot. Although they did not reveal their purpose in coming, the abbot told them, "It's not that I feel possessive of Atisha, but there are very few masters like him, and if he were to leave India, there would be a great danger to the Dharma itself and therefore to the entire populace.

His presence in India is very important." The Tibetan translator was at last able to see Atisha, and his eyes filled with tears. Atisha noticed this and told him, "Do not worry. I know of the great sacrifice made by the Tibetan king on my account. I am seriously considering his request, but I am an old man and I also have the responsibility of looking after the monastery." But Atisha eventually agreed to come to Tibet. After his arrival in western Tibet, he was requested by the king's nephew to compose a text that would benefit the entire Buddhist teaching in Tibet. He has left us *The Lamp on the Path to Enlightenment,* which condenses all of the essential paths from the entire corpus of teachings into a form suitable to the actual needs of the Tibetan people.

In the early fifteenth century, the Tibetan teacher Tsong-kha-pa wrote a book called *Lam Rim* or *Stages of the Path to Enlightenment.* He elaborated on Atisha's presentation and made these integrated teachings more accessible for anyone to practice. The *Lam Rim* is the basis for the teaching contained in this book.

By showing all the stages of the path to enlightenment, the *Lam Rim* also shows how all the teachings are integral—how the Dharma includes both sutra, the common path, and tantra, the secret path. Although these teachings might appear at times to be contradictory, they are without contradiction when practiced appropriately in a gradual process. All of them are important as guides for the path to enlightenment. Some people think that they can undertake esoteric practices without understanding the basic Buddhist teachings. Without the proper foundation of the common path, one can make no progress in tantra at all. Without the compassionate wish to gain enlightenment in order to lead everyone to freedom, tantra just becomes some mantra recitation; tantric practice will be confined to playing instruments like cymbals and thigh-bone trumpets and making a lot of noise. The Perfection of Wisdom Sutra says that the practice of generosity, ethics, patience, effort, concentration, and wisdom are the only path, whether sutra or tantra, that all the Buddhas of the past traversed to enlightenment. If you give up the common aspects of the path, it is a great mistake.

Therefore, the great master Tsong-kha-pa, the author of the *Stages of the Path to Enlightenment*, advises that practitioners seek the guidance of an experienced spiritual master and strive to perceive all the teachings of the Buddha as appropriate and relevant to their practice. Those aspects that cannot immediately be put into practice should not be abandoned. Instead, ask inwardly that you may be able to put them into practice in the future. If you are able to do that, then your perspective on the Buddha's teachings will be very profound.

The entire Buddhist canon is necessary and relevant to a practitioner. When someone is painting a thangka (a Tibetan Buddhist scroll), the artist must appreciate the need for all types of paint. But that is not enough; he or she should know when each type of paint is needed, first painting the outline and then adding the colors. It is very important to know their actual sequence. Similarly, we must know the importance of all the Buddha's teachings as well as when and how they should be practiced. When these factors are present, all obscurations and difficulties associated with your practice will be naturally eliminated.

When I talk about the practice of the Dharma, I do not mean leaving everything behind and going into isolated retreat. I simply mean that we should integrate a higher level of awareness into our daily lives. Whether we are eating or sleeping or doing business, we should constantly check our intentions, check our body, speech, mind, and actions, for even the subtlest negativity. Try to bring your day-to-day activities into line with a compassionate motivation. Infuse your acts of body, speech, and mind with the wisdom gained from hearing the teachings and from practice. But if someone is capable of giving up everything and devoting his or her life to practice, that person is worthy of admiration.

Study is like the light that illuminates the darkness of ignorance, and the resulting knowledge is the supreme possession because it cannot be taken by even the greatest of thieves. Study is the weapon that eliminates the enemy of ignorance. It is also the best friend to guide us through all our difficult times. We gain true friends by having a kind heart and not deceiving people. The friends that we make when we have power, position, and influence are friends based only upon our power, influence, and position. When we meet with misfortune and lose our wealth, these so-called friends leave us behind. The infallible friend is study of the teachings. This is a medicine that has no side effects or dangers. Knowledge is like the great army that will help us crush the forces of our own faults. With that knowledge we can protect ourselves from committing nonvirtuous actions. Fame, position, and wealth may result from one's knowledge; but only study and practice dedicated to removing delusion brings the enduring happiness of enlightenment.

Without the knowledge of the teachings, realizations will not follow. The teachings we receive are meant to be lived. When we train a horse for a race, it should be on the same kind of track on which the race will be run. Similarly, the topics that you have studied are the very teachings you should put into practice. Study is undertaken for the sake of practice. Tsong-kha-pa says that if you are able to perceive the profound and extensive sutras as personal advice, then you will not have any difficulties in perceiving the tantras and their commentaries as personal advice to be put into practice in the process of the path leading to enlightenment. This protects us from the misconception that some sets of teachings are not necessary for practice and some sets of teachings are necessary only for scholastic achievement.

Bowing down and folding our hands before receiving teachings is a way of countering pride and conceit. Sometimes you see people who know less about the

Dharma than you do but who have a greater sense of humility and respect. As a result of your knowledge of the Dharma, you should be more humble than the other person. If you are not, then it is you who are inferior to that person. So when you study, try to check your own state of mind and integrate what you study into your way of thinking. If that is undertaken, you will reach a stage where you will be able to see some kind of effect, some change or impact within your mind. That is an indication that you are making progress in your practice and that the purpose of study has been fulfilled.

Conquering the delusions is the task of a lifetime. If we are able to engage in practice in a sustained manner, then over the months and years we will see a transformation of the mind. But if we look for instant realization or instant taming of thoughts and emotions, then we will become discouraged and depressed. The eleventh-century yogi Milarepa, one of the greatest masters in Tibetan history, spent years living like a wild animal and undergoing great hardship in order to be able to achieve high realizations. If we were able to devote this kind of time and energy, then we would be able to see more quickly the benefit resulting from our practice.

So long as we have any belief in the efficacy of the teachings, it is important to develop conviction in the value of engaging in practice right away. In order to progress along the path, it is important to gain proper understanding of the path, and that can be achieved only by listening to a teaching. So develop a motivation to achieve the completely enlightened state for the sake of all other sentient beings, and with that motivation listen to or read this teaching.

When someone teaches the Dharma, he or she is serving as the messenger of the Buddhas. Regardless of the actual realization of the master, it is important for the listener to regard the teacher as inseparable from the Buddha. Listeners should not be spending time reflecting upon the faults of the master. In the Jataka Tales it is said that one should sit on a very low seat, and with a tamed mind and with great pleasure look at the face of the master and drink the nectar of his or her words, just as patients would attentively listen to the words of the doctor. The Buddha said that one should not rely upon the person of the master but rather rely upon the teaching, the substance of his or her teaching, the message of the Buddha. It is very important to respect the teacher from the viewpoint of the sacredness of the teaching itself.

When listening to or reading teachings, we are like a vase meant to collect wisdom. If the vase is upside down, though the gods might rain down nectar, it would merely drain down the sides of the vase. If the vessel is dirty, the nectar would be spoiled. If the vase has a hole in it, the nectar would leak out. Although we might attend a teaching, if we are easily distracted, we are like a vessel turned upside down. Though we might be attentive, if our attitude is dominated by negative intentions, like listening to the teaching in order to prove superior intelligence, we are like a dirty vessel. Finally, although we may be free from these faults, if we do not take them to heart, it is like letting the teachings in through one ear and out the other. After the teaching is over we will be totally blank, as though we could not take the teaching past the door when we left. This is why it is a good idea to take notes or, nowadays, use a tape recorder. The ability to retain the teachings depends upon the force of familiarity.

In a discussion with Khun-nu Lama, he vividly narrated events from his life that had taken place long before I was born. I am now fifty-nine. I tend to forget even the texts I am studying at the moment. Khun-nu Lama said that not studying constantly is due to the fault of not having joyous effort, and I think this is very true. Because of my lack of time I do not read a text often; I just read it through once and then get some kind of overall idea of what it is about. Because I have relatively good intelligence I read texts very quickly but do not read them often. As the saying goes, the person with great intelligence is like a burning field: the fire swiftly passes away.

If you read Tsong-kha-pa's *Stages of the Path to Enlightenment* nine times you will have nine different understandings of the text. When you read a newspaper article once, there is often no point in reading it again; you do not enjoy it, you just feel bored. When you read profound and eloquently written texts for the second, third, and fourth times, you sometimes feel surprised that you missed this or that point, although you have read it many times before. Sometimes you get a new understanding and different perspective, so constant familiarity is the main method for not forgetting. Those who wish to achieve omniscience should be single-pointed, attentive, and mentally humble, motivated by a wish to help other sentient beings, paying full attention with their minds, looking at the spiritual master with their eyes, and listening to the spiritual master with their ears.

It is also important to listen to teachings with a proper attitude. First, you should recognize yourself as a patient and the teacher as the doctor. The great Indian poet Shantideva says that when we are afflicted by ordinary illnesses, we have to follow the word of the doctor. Since we are afflicted by hundreds of illnesses caused by delusions like desire and hatred, there is no question that we should follow the word of a teacher. Delusions are very insidious. When a delusion like anger is present, we lose control. Worries due to attachment keep us from sleeping or enjoying a meal. Just as the patient would treat the medicines given by the doctor as very precious, taking care not to waste them, in the same manner teachings given by a spiritual master should be preserved as precious.

In order for the patient to get rid of the illness, he or she has to take medicine. Just simply having medicine in a bottle will not help. Similarly, in order to free our minds from the chronic disease of delusions, we have to put the teachings into practice, and it is only through practice that we will be able to free ourselves of the disease of delusion. Even over the short term, the greater the force of your patience, the less will be your anger and the greater the force of your respect for others. As your pride and conceit diminish, the influence of the delusions slowly decreases. Tsong-kha-pa says that someone suffering from the chronic disease of leprosy cannot get rid of it by taking medicine once or twice; it has to be taken continuously. In the same way, our minds have been under the constant grip of delusions since beginningless time. How can we expect to free them simply by undertaking practice once or twice? How can we expect to cure an illness by simply reading a medical text?

Within Tibetan Buddhism there are four schools: Nyingma, Sakya, Geluk, and Kagyu. It is a great mistake to claim that one of these schools is superior to the others. They all follow the same master, the Buddha Shakyamuni; they have all combined the systems of sutra and tantra. I try to cultivate a faith and admiration for all the four schools. I do it not just as a diplomatic gesture, but out of strong conviction. It also befits my position as Dalai Lama to know enough about the teachings of all four schools to be able to offer advice to those who come to me. Otherwise, I am like a mother with no arms watching a child drown. There was a Nyingma meditator who once came and asked me about a certain practice that I did not know well. I was able to send him to a great master who could answer his question, but I felt depressed that he had come sincerely seeking a teaching from me and I could not fulfill his wish. It is one thing if another's wish is beyond one's ability to fulfill, but so long as it is within one's own ability, it is very important to meet the spiritual needs of as many sentient beings as possible. We must study all the aspects of the teachings and develop admiration for them.

Nor should we consider Tibetan Buddhism to be superior to other forms of Buddhism. In Thailand, Burma, and Sri Lanka the monks have a true commitment to the practice of monastic discipline, and, unlike Tibetan monks, they still maintain the custom of begging for meals, which was practiced 2,500 years ago by the Buddha and his disciples. In Thailand I joined a group of monks on their rounds. It was a hot, sunny day, and because the tradition is to go without shoes, my feet really burned. Apart from that it was inspiring to see the practice of the Thai monks.

These days many people see only negativity in the practice of a spiritual tradition or religion. They see only how religious institutions exploit the masses and take away their possessions. However, the faults they see are not faults of the traditions themselves, but of the persons who claim to be followers of such traditions, like the members of monasteries or churches who use spiritual excuses for bettering themselves at the expense of other adherents. If spiritual practitioners themselves are careless, it reflects on everyone involved in that practice. Attempts to correct institutionalized faults are often misconstrued as an attack on the tradition as a whole. Many people conclude that religion is harmful and cannot help them. They reject any form of faith. Others are totally indifferent to spiritual practice and are satisfied with their worldly way of life. They have physical and material comforts and are neither for nor against religion. Yet all are equal in that they have the instinctive wish to gain happiness and avoid suffering.

If we abandon spiritual practice, or in this case Buddhism, we no longer give credence to the law of karma and will cease to perceive our misfortunes as the consequence of past negative actions. They appear perhaps as manifestations of faults within society or the community or the result of the action of a friend. We then go about blaming others for things that may even seem clearly to be our own fault. This blaming will reinforce self-centered attitudes, like attachment and hatred. Through association with such deluded attitudes, we become attached to our belongings and beset by mistrust or even paranoia. The Chinese Communists abandoned religion for the sake of what they saw as liberation. They call each other comrade and in the past made great sacrifices in the struggle for the liberation of their country. But after gaining power, they created political rivalries and now often fight against each other. One tries to take advantage of the other, and eventually one destroys the other. Although socialism has the noble aim of working for the common welfare of the masses, the means for achieving that end have antagonized the community, and the attitude of the people has become confrontational. In this form,

Communism has become so destructive that all the energy of the government is directed toward repression rather than liberation.

In contrast to the Communists, many great practitioners have traveled the Buddhist path and led their lives on the basis of love and compassion. With such motives your basic intention would be to work for the benefit of sentient beings, for whose sake you are trying to cultivate positive states of mind. Even if the damage done by the Chinese Communists in Tibet and China had been matched by an equally extensive positive program, I doubt that they would have been able to contribute much to the betterment of society because they lack the motivation of great compassion. When we look at Karl Marx's own life and the actual origin of Marxism, we find that Karl Marx underwent great sufferings during his lifetime and advocated constant struggle to topple the bourgeois class. His outlook was based on confrontation. Because of that primary motive, the entire movement of Communism has failed. If the primary motive had been based on compassion and altruism, then things would have been very different.

Many who are indifferent to any form of spiritual practice are materially well off in some developed countries, but even then they are completely unsatisfied. Although they are affluent they are not content. They suffer the anguish of wanting more, so that although they are materially wealthy, they are mentally poor. It is when they find that they cannot achieve whatever they wish for that the trouble really starts. They become depressed and anxiety creeps in. I have talked with some of my friends who are very wealthy, but because of their material outlook on life, they are absorbed by business and make no room for a practice, which might help them gain some perspective. In the process they actually lose the dream of happiness, which money was to have provided.

In Buddhist practice, instead of avoiding these sufferings we deliberately visualize them—the sufferings of birth, the sufferings of aging, the sufferings of fluctuations in status, the sufferings of uncertainty within this lifetime, and the sufferings of death. We try deliberately to think of them so that when we actually do face them, we are prepared. When we meet with death, we will realize that our time has come. That does not mean that we would not protect our bodies. When we are sick we take medicines and try to avert death. But if death is unavoidable, then the Buddhist will be prepared. Let us set aside for the moment the question of life after death, liberation, or the omniscient state. Even within this lifetime, thinking about the Dharma and belief in the Dharma has practical benefits. In Tibet, although the Chinese have meted out such systematic destruction and torture, the people still have not lost their hope and their determination. I think it is because of the Buddhist tradition.

Although the destruction of Buddhism has not gone on as long under Chinese rule as it did under Lang-dar-ma in the ninth century, the extent of destruction is far greater. When Lang-dar-ma had destroyed the Dharma, it was Atisha who came to Tibet and restored the entire practice of Buddhism. Now, whether we are capable or not, the responsibility has fallen on all of us to restore that which has been systematically destroyed by the Chinese. Buddhism is a treasure meant for the entire world. To teach and to listen to this teaching is a contribution to the wealth of humanity. There might be many points that you are not able to practice immediately, but keep them in your heart so that you will be able to practice them next year or after five or ten years, as long as the teachings are not forgotten.

Although we exiled Tibetans are struck by the tragedy of losing our country, we remain generally free from obstacles in the practice of the Dharma. In whatever country we reside, we have access to the Buddha's teachings through exiled teachers, and we know how to create conditions conducive to meditation. Tibetans have been doing this since at least the eighth century. Those who remained in Tibet after the 1959 Chinese invasion have had to undergo great physical and mental suffering. Monasteries were emptied, great teachers were imprisoned, and the practice of Buddhism became punishable by imprisonment or even death.

We must use all opportunities to practice the truth, to improve ourselves, instead of waiting for a time when we think we will be less busy. As Gung-thang Rinpoche said, the activities of this world are like ripples on a pond: when one disappears another emerges;

there is no end to them. Worldly activities do not stop until the time of death; we should try to search for a time within our own daily lives to practice the Dharma. At this juncture—when we have obtained the precious human form and have met with the Dharma and have some faith in it—if we are not able to put the Dharma into practice, it will be difficult for us to undertake its practice in future lifetimes, when we will not have such conditions. Now that we have met with such a profound system, in which the entire method for the achievement of the enlightened state is accessible, it would be very sad if we did not try to make the Dharma have some impact on our lives.

CHAPTER 2

THE TEACHER

Infinite numbers of Buddhas have appeared in the past, and we have not had the fortune of meeting them. Buddha Shakyamuni

came to care for the sentient beings of this degenerate time. He appeared in this world 2,500 years ago and has since shown many sentient beings the path to freedom from the cycle of suffering. We, however, did not have the fortune to meet him and come under his guidance and so are left with untamed, ordinary minds. There have been many great masters in India and in Tibet who achieved the completely enlightened state. Many other great masters have achieved high realizations, while others just managed to enter the path.

The teachings have been present for many centuries now, but what is important about the presence of the Dharma is not its continuity over time, but whether or not it is present in our own minds, whether it is alive in our actions. If we are satisfied merely that the teaching of the Buddha still exists in the world, then there is danger of its deteriorating because no one will be able to speak from the experience of practice. After the passing away of the Thirteenth Dalai Lama in 1933, the Tibetans isolated themselves. Despite the great transformation taking place in other parts of the world, Tibetans shut themselves in and left themselves open to invasion by the Chinese. Tibetan Buddhism is now vulnerable to degeneration since the dispersal of the Tibetans, so it is very important to really put effort into the practice of the Dharma at this time. At such critical moments, it is the spiritual master who protects us and sustains us. It is the guru who introduces us to the vast and profound teachings set forth by the Buddha himself in a manner suited to our understanding.

Although all the Buddhas are actively engaged in working for the benefit of other sentient beings, whether or not we will be able to enjoy such benefits depends upon how we relate to our spiritual master. The spiritual master is the only door to enlightenment because he or she is the living teacher to whom we can relate directly. Meeting with a spiritual master is not enough if we do not follow the advice given about practice and how to lead our lives. If we have the good fortune to encounter these teachings, it means that we are free from most of the major obstacles to the practice of the Dharma, so it is important to make the remaining part of our lives meaningful by engaging in spiritual practice. If we take the initiative now, the likelihood is that we will be able to progress along the path.

The practice of any path should be based on comprehensive and authentic instructions. We must consider carefully what kind of practice we would like to undertake and what kind of teachings we want to base our practice on. The great Tibetan scholar Sakya Pandita (1182–1251) used to say that people take great care over worldly matters like buying a horse. Thus when you are choosing to practice the Dharma it is important to be even more selective about the practice and the teacher, because the goal is Buddhahood, not transportation. Whether or not the teacher is authentic does not depend upon on the ability to quote from Buddhist texts. You should analyze his or her words and actions. Through constant close analysis you will be able to develop deep admiration for that person.

The Tibetan master Po-to-wa (1031–1106) said that the starting point of the entire path is learning to take the advice of a spiritual master and that the slightest experience of realization and the slightest diminishment in delusion all come as a consequence of the teachings of the spiritual master. If we cannot manage our affairs without the guidance of a good lawyer, there is no question of the importance of a spiritual master if we are to follow the unfamiliar path to Buddhahood.

There are cases of people with great intelligence who seem to be very clever, but the moment they direct their attention toward the Dharma their minds become numb. This indicates that they have not accumulated sufficient positive potential. There are also cases of people who are very intelligent and have great knowledge of the Dharma, but this knowledge does not affect their minds. They do not put what they know into practice. In this context, the spiritual master is very important. High realization especially can be gained only through the gradual guidance of a spiritual master who has authentic experience. The teacher becomes a role model and source of inspiration for our practice. It is possible to develop strong conviction by reading texts related to the practice of compassion, but when we meet a living person who has practiced it and who can teach us the practice of compassion from his or her own experience, it inspires us more powerfully.

Tsong-kha-pa says that unless the mind of the teacher is tamed, there is no hope of the teacher's taming others. Teachers should be restrained in their demeanor; their minds should be protected from distractions by the power of concentration. They should be equipped with the faculty of wisdom, penetrating the appearance of phenomena. If one possesses higher training in ethical discipline, one's mind is said to be tamed. In the Pratimoksha Sutra, the sutra dealing with monastic vows, the mind is compared to a wild horse, and the practice of ethics is compared to the reins by which this wild horse is tamed. So when the untamed mind departs from the path and indulges in negative actions, this wild horse should be tamed by using the rein of ethics, restraining the body and mind from negative actions.

A qualified teacher must also be skilled in the higher training of concentration evidenced by the constant application of mindfulness and introspection. Those who have lived recently in Tibet have gained great experience in the application of mindfulness and introspection, because even the slightest physical expression of dissent angers the Chinese regime. They have to be constantly mindful and alert to whether they are transgressing some rule. A teacher must also be completely pacified by the higher training in the wisdom of understanding the illusionlike nature of phenomena.

Tsong-kha-pa says that having only tamed one's mind is not sufficient; one should have knowledge of the teachings as well. The lama Drom-ton-pa (1005–1064) used to say that when a great teacher speaks on one specific topic, he or she should be able to relate it to the entire canon of the path to Buddhahood. Teachers should be able to turn their understanding of an entire topic into an instruction that is beneficial and easy to apply. Just as the scriptures say, the Buddhas cannot wash away the negative actions of others, nor can they remove the sufferings of others, nor can they transfer their realizations to us. It is only by showing the right path for us to follow that the Buddhas can liberate sentient beings.

The very purpose of teaching others is to help them understand. Therefore, it is important to have an appealing style of speaking, to do what is necessary to get the point across. The motive for teaching should be pure—never done out of a wish for fame or material gain. If money is the motive, then the teaching becomes merely a worldly activity. Before the Chinese came in 1951, some people in Lhasa either read texts or sang songs in order to collect money. It still happens in Tibet. Tourists gather around and take pictures. I think this is quite sad, because the Dharma is being used as an instrument for begging, not for spiritual advancement.

Po-to-wa said that although he had given many teachings he had never mentally accepted even the slightest compliment, because he was teaching out of his compassion for other sentient beings. He regarded it as his responsibility to teach because his primary purpose was to help others. There is no point in making others feel indebted or in accepting their thanks, because what you are actually doing is fulfilling your own pledge. When you eat your own food, there is no point in thanking yourself, because eating is something you have to do.

Tsong-kha-pa says that the spiritual masters who serve as guides on the path of enlightenment are like the foundation or root of your achievement of enlightenment. Therefore, those seeking a spiritual master should be familiar with the necessary qualifications and determine whether the teacher has those qualifications. In the world, without a proper leader we cannot improve our society. Similarly, unless the spiritual master is properly qualified, despite your strong faith, following him or her could be harmful if you are led in the wrong direction. Therefore, before actually taking someone as a spiritual master it is important to examine him or her, ask others about that person, and examine yourself. When you find that a person is suitable to be a spiritual master, only then should you start regarding him or her as your spiritual master. Likewise, before the spiritual master accepts someone as a disciple, it is very important that he or she first completely fulfill the qualifications of a spiritual master.

Just because a lama has some attendants or servants does not qualify him as a spiritual master. There is a difference between being a spiritual master and being a tulku, or the reincarnation of a particular master who has been returning for generations. There are some who are both, some are tulkus but not lamas, and some are lamas but not tulkus. Within the Tibetan community tulkus occupy a high position. If they do not also have the qualities of a spiritual master, then theirs is merely social status. Within Tibetan society, and even in the West where many lamas have gone to teach, when someone is called a tulku, people immediately look up to him. But others, who are really serious practitioners, do not command much respect simply because they do not have the label tulku. The greatest Buddhist philosopher of India, Nagarjuna, is regarded as a master by all later practitioners, although he had a simple name and we have no record of his having had an entourage or private secretary. Our Tibetan lamas have long and grand-sounding names, some of which are difficult to pronounce. In fact, there is no need to have a title other than that of bhikshu (monk), which was given by the Buddha himself. These are some of the great mistakes of Tibetan society. We Tibetans do not pay attention to the yellow monastic robes actually given by the Buddha himself but instead pay more attention to garments that are given as a mark of rank to make the person look grand. Later Indian masters wore some kind of reddish hat, and in Tibet their followers became more attentive to that red hat than to what was truly important.

The importance of finding a trustworthy teacher cannot be overemphasized, and I think Tibet's own political situation shows the folly of not being skeptical of a leader. Under the guise of being sponsors and benefactors, the Chinese established a close relationship with Tibet. We did not realize that China did so in order to portray Tibet as a province of its own country and would eventually use that argument to justify invasion. If we do not manage our affairs both spiritually and socially in a responsible manner, we will inevitably come to regret it later.

The great monk Geshe Sang-pu-wa (twelfth century) had many spiritual masters. Once, when he was traveling from eastern Tibet, he met a lay disciple giving teachings. Geshe Sang-pu-wa went to listen. When his attendants asked why he needed to go to take teachings from a layman, Geshe Sang-pu-wa replied that he had heard two points that were very helpful. Because Geshe Sang-pu-wa was able to develop admiration for and faith in many people, it was not a problem for him to have many teachers. People like us, whose minds are not yet tamed, are likely to see faults in our spiritual master and are prone to lose faith easily. So long as we see faults in the spiritual master and so long as we are prone to lose faith as a result of seeing superficial or projected faults, it is better to have fewer spiritual masters but to relate to them well. If you do not have this problem, you are free to have as many spiritual masters as possible.

When you see the spiritual master as the embodiment of all the Buddhas and take refuge, that faith is based on admiration. When you cultivate faith by perceiving the guru as the foundation and the root of your development, that is faith based on conviction. When you develop faith in the spiritual master by following his or her words, that is called aspiring faith. Generally speaking, faith is said to be the root or foundation of all virtuous thoughts. When you are able to see your spiritual master as equal to the Buddha himself, you will be able to stop yourself from seeing your spiritual master's faults and will perceive only his or her great qualities. But faith must be based on tried and tested experience. Therefore, you should constantly and deliberately try to prevent the kind of perceptions that lead you to see faults in the spiritual master, which actually might be your own projections, and try to see great qualities within the spiritual master. It is said that although your spiritual master may not be a true Buddha in reality, if you view the spiritual master as an actual Buddha, then you will obtain inspiration as if from an actual Buddha. On the other hand, even though your spiritual master might be a perfect Buddha in reality, if you are not able to view him or her in that way, you will receive the inspiration of an ordinary human being.

At this time, in this age of degeneration, gurus work on behalf of all the Buddhas and bodhisattvas in order to liberate all sentient beings from the cycle of suffering. It is prophesied in many tantras that in the degenerate age, the Buddha will appear in the world in the form of gurus. And in the degenerate age, their compassion must work in a more forceful manner, which can be confusing to those who expect compassion to take a certain form. If we are not receptive to the Buddha's teaching and compassion, then no teacher can help us much. But faith and conviction will open us to the power of the Buddhas, whose strong compassion is directed toward all sentient beings without exception. That includes you and me.

One teaching says, "While I was wandering in the cycle of existence, you [the Buddha] searched for me and illuminated my ignorance. You have shown me the light and released me from bondage." We can find the Buddha who is working for us by a process of elimination. Ask yourself who, among those close to you, is leading you out of the cycle of suffering caused by ignorance, attachment, and hatred. Is it one of your parents? Your friends? Your husband or wife? Your friends do not, your relatives do not, your parents do not. So if there is a Buddha working for you, he or she must be the person in your life leading you to enlightenment—your teacher. That is how one can view the teacher as the perfect Buddha. There have been cases in the past where, due to a mental obstruction, practitioners saw the actual Buddha in ordinary form. Asanga (fourth century C.E.) had a vision of the Buddha of the future, Maitreya, as a maggot-ridden dog, and Sang-pu-wa saw a female Buddha as an old leper woman. If we were to meet the great masters of the past who achieved enlightenment within one lifetime, they would look just like ordinary Indian beggars who wander around naked with lines painted on their foreheads.

When I speak of the importance of devotion to the teacher and of perceiving him or her as the Buddha, please do not misconstrue it to mean that I am implying that I am a Buddha. This is not the case; I know I am not a Buddha. Whether I am exalted or condemned, I will still be the ordinary Buddhist monk that I am. I am a monk, and I find it very comfortable. People call me the Bodhisattva of Compassion, Avalokiteshvara, but that does not make me Avalokiteshvara. The Chinese call me a wolf wearing a yellow robe, but that does not make me less of a human being or more of a wolf. I just remain an ordinary monk.

What should you do if following the instructions of your master causes you to act immorally or if his or her teachings contradict the Buddhist teachings? You should adhere to what is virtuous and leave what is not in conformity with the Dharma. In India there was once a teacher with many disciples who asked them to go out and steal. The teacher was a member of the brahmin caste and was very poor. He told them that when brahmins become poor they have a right to steal. As favorites of the god Brahma, the creator of the world, he said, it would not be nonvirtuous for a brahmin to steal. The disciples were about to go on their thieving expedition, when the brahmin noticed that one student stood in silence with his head bowed. The brahmin asked him why he was not moving. The student said, "What you have advised us to do now goes against the Dharma, so I do not think I can do it." This pleased the brahmin who said, "I tested your knowledge. Although you have all been my pupils and are loyal to me, the difference between you is in your judgment. This boy is very loyal to me, but when I advised something wrong, he was able to recognize that it went against the Dharma and would not do it. That is correct. I am your teacher, but you must examine my advice, and whenever it goes against the Dharma you should not follow it."

CHAPTER 3

THE OPPORTUNITY

Imagine a wide ocean with a golden yoke
adrift upon it. In the depths of the ocean
swims a single blind turtle, who

surfaces for air once every hundred years. How rare
would it be for the turtle to surface with its head
through the hole in the yoke? The Buddha said that
attaining a precious human rebirth is rarer than that.

It is said that even the gods envy our human existence, because it is the best form of existence for the
practice of the Dharma. There are something like five
billion people in this world, and all of them are human
beings. Their hands, brains, limbs, and bodies are
quite the same. But if we examine whether all humans
have the opportunity for practice, then we will find a
vast difference. We are free from adverse circumstances
that prevent the practice of the Dharma, adverse circumstances such as rebirth with wrong views, rebirth
as an animal, ghost, a hell being, or as a god addicted
to pleasure, or as a human who has difficulty hearing
the teachings, or being born into a place where there is

no Buddhist teaching available. Other adverse circumstances would be to be born in a barbarous land where thoughts of survival consume all one's resources or at a time when no Buddha has appeared.

On the positive side, we are endowed with many things that make our practice possible. For example, we have been born as humans able to respond to the teachings in a land where the teachings are available. We have not committed any heinous crimes and have a degree of faith in the Buddhist teachings. Although we have not taken rebirth in the world when the Buddha was alive, we have met with spiritual masters who can trace the lineage of the teachings they have received all the way back to the Buddha. The Dharma remains stable and flourishing because there are practitioners following these teachings. We also live in a time when there are kind benefactors who provide monks and nuns with necessities for practice, such as food, clothing, and shelter.

The Buddha's teachings benefit infinite numbers of beings, who as a result of practice achieve high realizations and eliminate delusions from their minds. But if we have taken rebirth as an animal or hell being or hungry ghost [described in chapter 5], the presence of the Buddha's doctrine in this world will not help us at all. For example, the Buddha Shakyamuni was born in India, became completely enlightened, and turned the wheel of the Dharma three times. If we had obtained a precious human life at that time and had been cared for by the Buddha, then our present fate would be totally different. We might have escaped rebirth by this time. But that was not the case, and his teaching did not benefit us at all until now. It is fortunate that we are not in the lower forms of existence, but simply taking rebirth in a human form and being freed of the bondage of nonhuman existence is not enough. Suppose we had taken rebirth in a place where the Dharma flourishes, but if we were born without full mental faculties, the Dharma would not benefit us. Physical disabilities need not impede the practice of the Dharma, but without use of the mind, it would be impossible. Even if we had no disabilities, if we had been born into a community where they deny the law of cause and effect, our intellects would have been filled with wrong views. But that is not the case. If we had taken rebirth during the times when there was no Buddhist doctrine at all, then we would not be on a path of transforming the mind to end suffering. But that also is not the case. We should recognize the fortune of taking rebirth at a time when the Buddha's teachings exist. We should reflect on this, rejoicing in our fortune of being free from such disadvantages. When we think along such lines we will finally be able to realize that we have obtained a form of human existence that is unique. If we consider it in such a detailed manner, we will eventually recognize the real significance of human existence. We will decide to make a very strong commitment to a serious practice of the Dharma.

It is said that the doctrine of Buddha Shakyamuni will remain five thousand years. If we take rebirth as a human after that, we will not benefit from it. But we have taken rebirth in this world during an eon of illumination when the Buddha's doctrine still remains. In order to want to transform the mind, you must be persuaded to take full advantage of your life as a human.

Up to this point, we have been living our lives, we have been eating, we have found shelter, we have been wearing clothes. If we were to continue in this same manner, simply eating for the sake of living, what meaning does that give our lives? We have all obtained a precious human form, but simply obtaining a human form is nothing to be proud of. There are an infinite number of other forms of life on the planet, but none are engaged in the kind of destruction in which humans indulge. Human beings endanger all the life on the planet. If we let compassion and an altruistic attitude guide our lives, we will be able to achieve great things—something that other forms of life are not able to do. If we are able to use this precious human form in a positive manner, it will have value in the long term. Our human existence will then become truly precious. If, however, we use our human potential, the ability of the brain, in negative ways, to torture people, exploit others, and cause destruction, then our human existence will be a danger to ourselves in the future as well as to others right now. Human existence, if used destructively, has the potential to annihilate everything we know. Or, it can be the source for becoming a Buddha.

Up to now we have not made much headway in our spiritual progress. Ask yourself, "What wholesome deeds have I done so far; what practices have I done to tame the mind and make myself confident in the future?" If you do not find anything that would give you a sense of certainty about your future fate, then all this eating of food in order to maintain your life so far is pretty much a waste. As the eighth-century Indian poet Shantideva says, our taking birth would have been simply for the sake of giving pain and difficulty to our mother; it would have served no other purpose.

Shantideva says that having achieved such a precious human form, I would be stupid not to meditate and accumulate virtues. If out of laziness I still postpone practice, at the time of death I will be seized by great remorse and concern for the sufferings I will undergo in the lower forms of existence. If having obtained such a valuable human existence, we then waste it, it would be like going to the land of jewels and coming back empty-handed. Reflect upon the fact that all the great masters of the past who achieved enlightenment within one lifetime—Nagarjuna, Asanga, and great Tibetan masters like Milarepa—had just the same human life that we have obtained now. The only difference between us and them is that we lack their initiative. By meditating on the rarity of our circumstances, we can cultivate a similar motivation.

Though a dog may live in a place where the Dharma is flourishing, the dog cannot actively benefit from it.

Animals are even more strongly ruled by delusions and do not have our ability to choose between different kinds of behavior. They indulge more easily in negative actions and thoughts like hatred and desire and have more difficulty with virtuous actions. If I take rebirth as an animal or any form of lower existence, how will I have the chance to practice the Dharma? It is very difficult to accumulate virtues, and I would be continuously accumulating nonvirtuous actions, so that even after death I would be spinning in a chain reaction of constantly taking rebirth in the lower forms of existence. If it is the case that even a momentary negative action has the potential to cause rebirth in the lower forms of existence for innumerable eons, then as a result of the infinite numbers of nonvirtuous actions that I have accumulated in the past, how can I doubt that I will take rebirth in the lower forms of existence? Once you take rebirth in the lower realms of existence, even though the karma that caused that rebirth can be exhausted by the sufferings you undergo, there is hardly any hope for you to be freed from those lower realms because, in a vicious cycle, you will be indulging in negative actions, which will cause another, lower rebirth. Having reflected upon the difficulty of obtaining such a human existence, and reflecting upon the stupidity of wasting it, you should make the decision to make the best use of your life by undertaking the practice of the Dharma.

It is generally said by Buddhists that our ordinary human existence requires as its primary cause a pure observance of ethics in a former life. In addition, especially for the attainment of a human form with the capacity to practice the Dharma, it is very important that the single ethical deed be complemented with other actions like generosity and aspirational prayers in the previous lifetime. If you consider it, you will find that it is very rare that someone possess all these factors. By thinking about the rarity of its cause, you will realize how difficult it is to obtain a precious human form. And if you compare human existence to other types of existence, such as animals, there are far more animals and insects than there are humans. Even within the human existence, one whose life is endowed with the leisure and opportunity to practice the Dharma is really very rare. If you understand the importance of this precious human life, then all the other realizations will come naturally. If someone who has gold in his hand throws it away and then prays to get more gold tomorrow, he would be a laughingstock. In the same way, although we might be old and physically weak, we are far superior in our capacity to practice the Dharma than are other sentient beings. We can at least recite the mantra of the Bodhisattva of Compassion, OM MANI PADME HUM. Even if a person is at the point of death, he or she still has the ability to think and to cultivate virtuous thoughts.

The Buddha's activities—from the beginning of his cultivating the wish to help others to the accumulating of merit and his eventual achievement of enlightenment—were all done for the sake of other sentient beings. The welfare of other sentient beings is classified into two types: temporary welfare, which is the achievement of favorable rebirth, and ultimate welfare, which is the achievement of liberation and the omniscient state. All the teachings associated with the achievement of favorable rebirth in the future are said to belong to the category of small scope. When we talk of our ultimate aim, it is of two types: liberation from suffering, and omniscience. All the teachings related to the practice of achieving personal liberation are teachings of middle scope. For this purpose, practitioners of middle scope engage in the practice of ethics, concentration, and wisdom and then eliminate the delusions and achieve liberation from suffering and rebirth. All the teachings that outline the techniques for achieving the omniscience of Buddhahood, including both the sutra vehicle and the tantric vehicle, are teachings related to practitioners of great scope. A being of great scope is someone whose mind is motivated by great compassion for all other sentient beings and who wishes to achieve enlightenment for their sake. Thus one group can think only of a future life; these are people of small scope. People in the second group are not preoccupied with the concerns of the future life alone but are able to think of something more distant, liberation from rebirth; these are beings of the middle scope. Yet other people are not concerned only with their own welfare but are more courageous. They are concerned with the welfare also of other sentient beings, and these are the beings of great scope.

Tsong-kha-pa says that although we divide the practice into three types, the practice of initial scope, middle scope, and great scope, the two earlier ones are included in the practices of the great scope, because they are like preparations for the practice of great scope. When we train our minds to realize the importance of our precious human life and its rarity, we decide to take advantage of it. Our bodies, composed of flesh, blood, and bones, are like the banana tree, which has no core, and they are the source of all sorts of physical sufferings. Therefore, we should not be so concerned about our bodies. Instead, following the example of the great bodhisattvas, we should make our human birth meaningful and use our bodies for the benefit of other sentient beings.

In other words, precious and rare opportunities surround us, and we should recognize their value. We have obtained this precious human form, endowed with these special characteristics. If we were to waste it, simply indulging in trivial concerns and trivial deeds, it would be sad. Having realized the value of the precious human form, it is important to make the decision to capitalize on it and use it for the practice of the Dharma. Otherwise, there would hardly be any difference between our lives as human beings and those of animals.

CHAPTER 4

DEATH

The Buddha said that of all the different
times for plowing, autumn is the best, and
of all the different kinds of fuel for fire,

cow dung is the best, and of all the different kinds of awareness, awareness of impermanence and death is best. Death is certain, but when it will strike is uncertain. If we really face up to things, we do not know which will come first—tomorrow or death. We cannot be entirely sure that the old are going to die first and the young are going to remain behind. The most realistic attitude we can cultivate is to hope for the best but be prepared for the worst. If the worst does not happen, then everything is fine, but if it does occur, it will not strike us unawares. This applies also to the practice of the Dharma: be prepared for the worst, for none of us knows when we are going to die.

Every day we hear of death in the news or the death of a friend, someone we knew vaguely, or a relative. Sometimes we feel the loss, sometimes we almost rejoice, but we still somehow hang onto the idea that it will not happen to us. We think we are immune to impermanence, and so we put off spiritual practice (which might prepare us for death), thinking that we will have time in the future. When the time inevitably arrives, the only thing that we are left with is regret. We need to engage in practice right now so that no matter how soon death comes, we will be prepared.

When the time of death comes, no circumstances can prevent it. No matter what type of body you might have, no matter how impervious to sickness you might be, death will certainly strike. If we reflect upon the lives of the past Buddhas and bodhisattvas, they are now only a memory. Great Indian masters, like Nagarjuna and Asanga, made great contributions to the Dharma and worked for the benefit of sentient be-ings, but all that remains of them now is their names. The same applies to great rulers and political leaders. The stories of their lives are so vivid that they seem almost to be alive. When we go on a pilgrimage in India, we find places like the great monastery of Nalanda, where great masters like Nagarjuna and Asanga studied and taught. Now Nalanda lies in ruins. When we see the traces left by the great figures of his-tory, the ruins show us the nature of impermanence. As the ancient Buddhist aphorisms say, whether we go underground or into the sea or into space, we will never be able to avoid death. The members of our own family will sooner or later be separated from each other like a collection of leaves blown about by wind. Within the next month or two, some of us will begin to die, and others will die within a few years. In eighty or ninety years all of us, including the Dalai Lama, will have died. Then only our spiritual realizations will help us.

There is no one who after taking birth goes farther and farther away from death. Instead, we get closer and closer, like animals being led to the slaughter. Just as cowherds strike their cows and oxen and lead them back to the cow shed, so we, tormented by sufferings of birth, illness, aging, and death, move ever closer to the ends of our lives. Everything in this universe is subject to impermanence and will eventually disintegrate. As the Seventh Dalai Lama said, young people who look very strong and healthy but die young are actually masters teaching us about impermanence. Of all the people we know or have seen, none will remain in one hundred years. Death cannot be averted by mantras or by seeking refuge in a powerful political leader.

During the years of my life I have met so many people. They are now only objects of my memory. Nowadays I meet more new people. It is just like watching a drama; after performing their parts, people change their costumes and reappear. If we spend our short lives under the influence of desire and hatred, if for the sake of those short lives we increase our delusions, the harm that we will do is very long-term, because it will destroy our prospects for achieving ultimate happiness.

If sometimes we are not successful in trivial worldly matters, it does not matter much, but if we waste this precious opportunity afforded by human life, we will be letting ourselves down in the long term. The future is in our hands—whether we want to undergo extreme suffering by falling into the realms of nonhuman existence or whether we want to achieve higher forms of rebirth or whether we want to reach the state of enlightenment. Shantideva says that in this life we have the opportunity, we have the responsibility, we have the ability to decide and determine what our future lives will be. We should train our minds so that our lives will not be wasted—not even for a month or a day—and prepare for the moment of death.

If we can cultivate that understanding, our motivation for spiritual practice will come from within—the strongest motivational factor there is. Geshe Sha-ra-wa (1070–1141) said that his best teacher was meditation on impermanence. The Buddha Shakyamuni said in his first teaching that the basis of suffering was impermanence.

When faced with death, the best practitioners will be delighted, the midlevel practitioners will be well prepared for it, and even the lowest practitioners will have no regret. When we reach the last day of our lives, it is very important not to have even a twinge of regret, or the negativity we experience at the time of death could influence our next rebirth. The best way to make life meaningful is to undertake the path of compassion.

If you reflect upon death and impermanence, you will begin to make your life meaningful. You might think that because sooner or later you have to die, there is no point in trying to think about death now, for it will just make you depressed and worried. But awareness of death and impermanence can have great benefits. If our minds are gripped by the feeling that we are not subject to death, then we will never be serious in our practice and will never make headway on the spiritual path. The belief that you will not die is the greatest stumbling block to spiritual progress: you will not remember the Dharma, you will not follow the Dharma even though you may remember it, and you will not follow the Dharma purely even though you may follow it to a certain extent. If you do not contemplate death, then you will never take your practice seriously. Overcome by laziness, you will lack effort and momentum in your practice, and you will be beset by exhaustion. You will have great attachment to fame, material wealth, and prosperity. When we think so much of this life, we tend to work for those we like— our relatives and friends—and we strive to make them happy. Then when others try to harm them, we immediately label these others as our enemies. In this way delusions like desire and hatred increase like a river flooding in the summer. These delusions automatically induce us to indulge in all sorts of negative actions whose consequences will be rebirth in lower forms of existence in the future.

As a result of a small accumulation of merit, we have already obtained a precious human life. Any remaining merit will manifest as some relative degree of prosperity in this life. So the little capital that we have will already be spent, and if we are not accumulating anything new, it is like spending our savings without making a new deposit. If we simply exhaust our collection of merit, then sooner or later we will be plunged into a future life of even more intense suffering.

It is said that if we do not have a proper awareness of death, we will die in the grip of fear and regret. That feeling can send us into the lower realms. Many people avoid speaking about death at all. They avoid thinking the worst, so when it actually happens they are taken by surprise and are totally unprepared. Buddhist practice advises us not to ignore misfortunes but to acknowledge and confront them, preparing for them right from the beginning, so that when we actually experience the suffering it is not completely unbearable. Simply avoiding a problem does not help resolve it but in fact can make it worse.

Some people remark that Buddhist practice seems to emphasize suffering and pessimism. I think this is quite wrong. Buddhist practice actually strives to gain an everlasting peace—something that is inconceivable to an ordinary mind—and to get rid of sufferings once and for all. Buddhists are not satisfied by prosperity in this lifetime alone or the prospect of prosperity in future lives but instead seek an ultimate happiness. Now the basic Buddhist outlook is that since sufferings are a reality, simply mentally avoiding them will not resolve the problem. What should be done is to confront suffering, face it and analyze it, examine it, determine its causes, and find out how best you can cope with it. When those who avoid thinking about misery are actually struck by it, they are unprepared and suffer more than those who have familiarized themselves with sufferings, their origin, and how they arise. A practitioner of the Dharma thinks daily about death, reflects upon the sufferings of human beings, the suffering at the time of birth, the suffering of aging, the suffering of sickness, and the suffering of death. Every day, tantric practitioners go through the death process in imagination. It is like mentally dying once every day. Because of their familiarity with it, they will be quite prepared when they actually meet with death. If you have to go through a very dangerous and frightening terrain, you should find out about the dangers and how to deal with them in advance. Not to think about them ahead of time would be foolish. Whether you like it or not you have to go there, so it is better to be prepared so that you will know how to react when the difficulties appear.

If you have a perfect awareness of death, you will feel certain that you are going to die soon. If you then find out that you are going to die today or tomorrow, because of your spiritual practice you will try to detach yourself from objects of attachment by getting rid of your belongings and seeing all worldly prosperity as without any essence or significance. You will try to put all your effort into your practice. The advantage of being aware of death is that it makes life meaningful, and, feeling delight when the time of death approaches, you will die without any regret.

When you reflect upon the certainty of death in general and the uncertainty of its time, you will make all effort to prepare yourself for the future. You will realize that the prosperity and activities of this life are without essence and unimportant. Then, working for the long-term benefit of yourself and others will seem much more important, and your life will be guided by that understanding. Just as Milarepa said, since sooner or later you have to leave everything behind, why not give it up right now? In spite of all our efforts, including taking medicines or doing long-life ceremonies, it is very unlikely that anyone will live more than one hundred years. There are some exceptional cases, but after sixty or seventy years most of the people reading this book will not be alive. After one hundred years people will reflect upon our time as simply a part of history.

When death arrives, the only thing that can help is the compassion and understanding of the nature of reality one has thus far gained. In this regard it is very important to examine whether or not there is life after death. Past and future lives exist for the following reasons. Certain patterns of thinking from last year, the year before that, and even from childhood can be recollected now. This clearly shows that there existed an awareness prior to the present awareness. The first instant of consciousness in this life is also not produced without a cause, nor is it born from something permanent or inanimate. A moment of mind is something that is clear and knowing. It must therefore be preceded by something that is clear and knowing, a previous moment of mind. It is not feasible that the first moment of mind in this life could come from anything other than a previous lifetime.

Although the physical body may act as a secondary cause of subtle changes in the mind, it cannot be the primary cause. Matter can never turn into mind, and mind cannot turn into matter. Therefore, mind must come from mind. The mind of this present life comes from the mind of the previous life and serves as the cause of the mind of the next life. When you reflect upon death and are aware of it constantly, your life will become meaningful.

Realizing the great disadvantages of our instinctive grasping at permanence, we must counter it and be constantly aware of death so that we will be motivated to undertake the practice of the Dharma more seriously. Tsong-kha-pa says that the importance of the awareness of death is not confined to the initial stage alone. It is important throughout all the stages of the path; it is important at the beginning, in the middle, and also at the end.

The awareness of death that we must cultivate is not the ordinary, incapacitating fear of being separated from our loved ones and possessions. Rather, we must learn to fear that we will die without having put an end to the causes for taking rebirth in lower forms of existence and will die without having accumulated the necessary causes and conditions for favorable future rebirth. If we do not accomplish these two aims, then at the time of death we will be gripped by strong fear and remorse. If we spend our entire lives indulging in negative actions induced by hatred and desire, we cause harm not only temporarily but also in the long term, because we accumulate and store up a wide collection of causes and conditions for our own downfall in future lives. Fear of that will inspire us to make even our day-to-day lives into something meaningful. Having gained an awareness of death, we will see the prosperity and affairs of this life as unimportant and will work for a better future. That is the purpose of meditating on death. If we fear death now, we will try to look for a method to overcome our fear and regret at the time of death. However, if we try to avoid a fear of death right now, at the time of death we will be gripped by remorse.

Tsong-kha-pa says that when our contemplation of impermanence becomes very firm and stable, everything we encounter will teach us about impermanence. He says that the process of approaching death starts right from conception and that when we are alive, our lives are constantly tormented by illness and aging. While we are healthy and alive we should not be lured into thinking that we will not die. We should not be obliviously delighted when we are well; it is better to be prepared for our future fate. For example, someone falling from a very high cliff is not happy before he or she hits the ground.

Even while we are alive there is very little time for the practice of the Dharma. Even if we assume that we might live long, perhaps a hundred years, we should never give in to the feeling that we will have time to practice the Dharma later. We should not be influenced by procrastination, which is a form of laziness. Half of one's life is spent in sleep, and for most of the rest of the time we are distracted by worldly activities. When we become old, our physical and mental strength decreases, and even though we might wish to practice, it will already be too late because we will not have the ability to practice the Dharma. Just as a scripture says, half of one's life is spent in sleep, for ten years we are children and twenty years we are old, and the time in between is tormented by worries, sorrow, suffering, and depressions, so there is hardly any time for the practice of the Dharma. If we live a life of sixty years and think of all the time we spend as children, all the time that we are asleep, and the time when we are too old, we will find that there are only about five years that we can devote to the serious practice of the Dharma. If we do not make a deliberate effort to undertake the practice of the Dharma but instead live as we normally do, we are certain to spend our lives in idleness without purpose. Gung-thang Rinpoche said, partly in jest, "I spent twenty years without thinking of practicing the Dharma and then I spent another twenty years thinking I would practice later and then I spent ten years thinking about how I had missed the chance to practice the Dharma."

When I was just a child, nothing much happened. At about fourteen or fifteen years of age, I began to take a serious interest in the Dharma. Then the Chinese came, and I spent many years in all sorts of political turmoil. I went to China and in 1956 I visited India. After that I returned to Tibet, and again some time was spent involved in political affairs. The best thing I can recall is my examination as a geshe [the highest academic degree in the Tibetan monastic universities], after which I had to leave my country. I have been in exile now for more than thirty years, and although I have managed some study and practice, most of my life is spent idly without much benefit. I have not yet reached the point of regretting that I have not practiced. If I think in terms of practicing Highest Yoga Tantra, there are certain aspects of the path that I cannot practice because my physical constituents have begun to deteriorate with age. The time for practicing the Dharma does not come naturally but has to be set aside deliberately.

If you must depart on a long journey, at a certain point it is necessary to make preparations. As I often like to say, we should spend 50 percent of our time and energy on the concerns of our future life and about 50 percent on the affairs of this lifetime.

There are many causes of death and very few causes of staying alive. Furthermore, those things that we normally regard as supporting life, such as food and medicine, can become causes of death. Many illnesses today are said to be caused by our diet. The chemicals used to grow crops and to raise animals contribute to bad health and cause imbalance within the body. The human body is so sensitive, so delicate, that if it is too fat, you have all sorts of problems: you cannot walk properly, you have high blood pressure, and your own body becomes a burden. On the other hand, if you are too thin, you have little strength or stamina, which leads to all sorts of other troubles. When you are young you worry about not being included among the grown-ups, and when you are too old you feel like you have been cast out of society. This is the nature of our existence. If the harm were some kind of externally inflicted thing, then you might somehow be able to avoid it; you could go underground or submerge yourself in the ocean. But when the harm comes from within, there is nothing much you can do. While we are free of illness and difficulty and we have a healthy body, we must capitalize on that and take the essence of it. To take the essence of life is to try to achieve a state that is totally free of illness, mortality, decay, and fear—that is, a state of liberation and omniscience.

The richest man in the world cannot take a single possession with him at death. Tsong-kha-pa says that if we must leave behind this body, which we have held so dear and labeled as our own and which has been accompanying us since our birth as our oldest companion, then there is no question of not leaving behind material belongings. Most people spend so much energy and time simply trying to gain some prosperity and happiness within this lifetime. But at the time of death, all our worldly activities, such as taking care of our relatives and friends and competing with our rivals, have to be left unfinished. Although you might have enough food to provide for one hundred years, at the time of death you will have to go hungry, and although you might have clothes that would suffice for one hundred years, at the time of death you will have to go naked. When death strikes there is no difference between the way a king dies, leaving his kingdom behind, and the way a beggar dies, leaving his stick behind.

You should try to imagine a situation in which you are sick. Imagine that you have a grave illness and your entire physical strength has gone; you feel exhausted, and even medicines will not help. When the time of death comes, the doctor will speak in two ways: to the patient he or she will say, "Don't worry, you will get better. There is nothing to worry about; just relax." To the family he or she will say, "The situation is very grave. You should arrange for the final ceremonies to be performed." At that time there will be no opportunity for you to complete unfinished business or to complete your studies. When you lie down your body will be so weak that you can hardly move. Then the heat of your body gradually dissolves and you feel that your body has become very stiff, like a tree that has fallen on your bed. You will actually begin to see your own corpse. Your last words will be barely audible, and the people around you will have to struggle to understand what you are saying. The last food you eat will

not be a delicious meal but a mixture of pills that you
will not have the strength to swallow. You will have to
leave your most intimate friends; it may be eons before
you meet them again. Your breathing pattern will
change and become noisy. Gradually it will become
more uneven, with the inhalation and exhalation coming faster and faster. Finally, there will be one last very
strong exhalation, and that will be the end of your
breath. That marks death as it is ordinarily understood. After that, your name, which once gave such delight to your friends and family when they heard it,
will have a prefix added to it, "the late."

It is crucial that at the time of death the mind is in a
virtuous state. It is the last chance that we have, and it
is a chance not to be missed. Although we might have
lived a very negative life, at the time of death we
should make great effort to cultivate a virtuous state of
mind. If we are able to develop a very strong and powerful compassion at the time of death, there is hope
that in the next life we will take rebirth in a favorable
existence. Generally speaking, familiarity plays a great
role in this. When people are sick and about to die, it is
unfortunate that others allow the dying person to feel
desire or hatred. At the very least the dying person
should be shown images of Buddhas and bodhisattvas
so that he or she can see them, try to develop strong
faith in them, and die in an auspicious frame of mind.
If this is not possible, it is very important that the attendants and relatives not make the dying person feel
upset. At that time a very strong emotion, like desire or

hatred, can send the person into a state of great suffering and quite possibly a lower rebirth.

As death approaches, certain signs indicating the future might appear. Those with virtuous minds will feel that they are going from darkness into light or onto open ground. They will feel happy, see visions of beautiful things, and will not feel any acute suffering as they die.

If at the time of death people have very strong feelings of desire or hatred, they will see all sorts of hallucinations and will feel great anxiety. Some people feel as if they are entering darkness; others feel that they are burning. I have met some people who had been very sick who told me that when they were seriously ill they had visions of being burned. This is an indication of their future fate. As a result of such signs, the dying person will feel very confused and will shout and moan, feeling as if the whole body is being pulled down. He or she will have acute pain at the time of death. All of this derives ultimately from attachment focused upon oneself. The dying know that the person they have cherished so much is going to die.

When those who have indulged most of their lives in negative action die, it is said that the process of the dissolution of the body's warmth starts from the upper part of the body until it reaches the heart. For practitioners of virtue it is said that the process of the dissolution of warmth starts from below, from the legs, and eventually reaches the heart. In any case, the consciousness actually departs from the heart.

After death one enters into the intermediate state, the bardo. The body in the intermediate state has several unique features: all the physical senses are complete, and it has a physical appearance that is identical to the physical appearance of the being that it will next take rebirth as. For example, if it is to take rebirth as a human being, it will have a physical appearance identical to a human being. If it is to take rebirth as an animal, then it will have the physical appearance of the particular animal. The being of the intermediate state has such powerful sight that it can see through solid objects and is able to travel anywhere without obstruction. Beings of the intermediate state are visible only to intermediate beings of the same type. For example, if an intermediate being is destined to be reborn as a human, it will be visible only to intermediate beings who are destined to take rebirth as humans. Intermediate beings of the god realm walk upward, looking upward, and the intermediate beings of the human realm walk straight and look straight. The intermediate beings of those who have indulged in negative actions and are destined to take rebirth in lower realms are said to move upside down.

The period of time spent in this intermediate state is seven days. After one week, if the intermediate-state being meets with appropriate circumstances, it will take rebirth in the appropriate realm of existence. If it does not, then it will again have to die a small death and arise as an intermediate being again. This can happen seven times, but after forty-nine days it can no longer remain as an intermediate-state being and must take rebirth, whether it likes it or not. When the time has come for it to take rebirth, it sees beings of its own type playing, and it will develop a wish to join them. The regenerative fluids of the future parents, the semen and the ovum, look different to it. Although the parents may not be actually sleeping together, the intermediate being will have the illusion that they are and will feel attachment to them. If someone is likely to be born as a girl, it is said she will feel repulsion for the mother and, driven by attachment, will try to sleep with the father. If someone is likely to be born as a boy, he will feel repulsion for the father but will have attachment to the mother and will try to sleep with her. Moved by such desire, he or she goes to where the parents are. Then, no part of the body of the parents appears to that being except for the sexual organs, and as a result the being feels frustrated and angry. That anger serves as the condition for its death from the intermediate state, and it takes rebirth in the womb. When the parents are copulating and achieve orgasm, it is said that one or two drops of thick semen and ovum mix together like cream on the surface of boiled milk. At that moment the consciousness of the intermediate being ceases and enters into the mixture. That marks the entry into the womb. Although the parents may not be copulating, the intermediate being has the illusion that they are doing so and will go to the place.

This implies that there are cases where, although the parents may not copulate, still consciousness can enter into the physical elements. This accounts for test-tube babies today; when the fluids are collected from the parents and are mixed and kept in a tube, the consciousness can enter into that mixture without actual copulation taking place.

Shantideva says that even animals work to experience pleasure and avoid pain in this life. We must turn our attention to the future; otherwise we will be no different from animals. Awareness of death is the very bedrock of the entire path. Until you have developed this awareness, all other practices are obstructed. The Dharma is the guide that leads us through unknown terrain; the Dharma is the food that sustains us in our journey; the Dharma is the captain that will take us to the unknown shore of nirvana. Therefore, put all the energy of your body, speech, and mind into the practice of the Dharma. To talk about meditation on death and impermanence is very easy, but the actual practice is really very difficult. And when we do practice, sometimes we do not notice much change, especially if we just compare yesterday and today. There is a danger of losing hope and becoming discouraged. In such situations, it is quite helpful not to compare days or weeks, but rather to try to compare our present state of mind with that of five years ago or ten years ago; then we will see that there has been some change. We may notice some change in our outlook, in our understanding, in our spontaneity, in our response to these practices.

That in itself is a source of great encouragement; it really gives us hope, because it shows that if we make the effort there is the potential for further progress. To become discouraged and decide to postpone our practice to a more favorable time is really very dangerous.

CHAPTER 5

REBIRTH

Karma can be understood as cause and effect
in much the same way that physicists
understand that for every action, there is

an equal and opposite reaction. As with physics, what form that reaction will take is not always predictable, but sometimes we can predict the reaction and we can do something to mitigate the outcome. Science is working on ways to clean up the environment now that it has been polluted, and many more scientists are attempting to prevent further pollution. In the same way, our future lives are determined by our present actions as well as those of our immediate past and past lives. The practice of the Dharma is meant to mitigate the outcome of our karmic actions and prevent any further pollution by negative thoughts and actions. Those negative thoughts and actions will otherwise land us in a rebirth of tremendous suffering. Sooner or later we are going to die, and so sooner or later we will have to take rebirth again. The realms of existence where we can take rebirth are confined to two, the favorable and the unfavorable. Where we take rebirth depends on karma.

Karma is created by an agent, a person, a living being. Living beings are nothing other than the self, imputed on the basis of the continuity of consciousness. The nature of consciousness is luminosity and clarity. It is an agent of knowing that is preceded by an earlier moment of consciousness that is its cause. If we come to understand that the continuity of consciousness cannot be exhausted within one lifetime, we will find that there is logical support for the possibility of life after death. If we are not convinced of the continuity of consciousness, at least we know that there is no evidence that can disprove the theory of life after death. We cannot prove it, but we cannot disprove it. There are many cases of people remembering their past lives vividly. It is not a phenomenon confined to Buddhists. There are people with such memories whose parents do not believe in life after death or past lives. I know of three cases of children who have been able to remember their past lives vividly. In one case the recollection of the past life was so vivid that even though the parents previously did not believe in life after death, as a result of the clarity of their child's recollections, they are now convinced. The child not only recollected clearly having lived in a nearby village that she recognized, but was able to identify her previous parents, whom she had no other occasion to know. If there is no life after death, there is no past life, and we will have to find another explanation for these recollections. There are also many cases of parents who have two children brought up in the same way, in the same society, with the same background, yet one is more successful than the other. We find that such differences come about as a result of differences in our past karmic actions.

Death is nothing other than the separation of the consciousness from the physical body. If you do not accept this phenomenon called consciousness, I think it is also very difficult to explain exactly what life is. When consciousness is connected to the body and their relationship continues, we call it life, and when consciousness terminates its relationship with a particular body, we call it death. Although our bodies are an aggregation of chemical or physical components, a kind of subtle agent of pure luminosity constitutes the life of living beings. Since it is not physical, we cannot measure it, but that does not mean that it does not exist. We have spent so much time, energy, and research in the exploration of the external world, but now if we change that approach and direct all this exploration, research, and energy inward and begin to analyze, I really think we have the ability to realize the nature of consciousness—this clarity, this luminosity—within ourselves.

According to the Buddhist explanation, consciousness is said to be nonobstructive and nonphysical, and it is from the actions of this consciousness that all emotions, all delusions, and all human faults arise. However, it is also because of the inherent nature of this consciousness that one can eliminate all these faults and delusions and bring about lasting peace and happiness. Since consciousness is the basis for existence and enlightenment, there are extensive writings on the topic.

We know from our own experience that consciousness or mind is subject to change, which implies that it is dependent upon causes and conditions that change, transform, and influence it: the conditions and circumstances of our lives. Consciousness must have a substantial cause similar to the nature of consciousness itself in order for it to arise. Without a prior moment of consciousness there cannot be any consciousness. It does not arise out of nothing, and it cannot turn into nothing. Matter cannot change into consciousness. Therefore, we should be able to trace the causal sequence of moments of consciousness back in time. The Buddhist scriptures speak of hundreds of billions of world systems, infinite numbers of world systems, and consciousness existing since beginningless time. I believe that other worlds exist. Modern cosmology also says that there are many different types of world systems. Although life has not been scientifically observed on other planets, it would be illogical to conclude that life is possible only on this planet, which is dependent upon this solar system, and not on other types of planets. Buddhist scriptures mention the presence of life in other world systems as well as different types of solar systems and an infinite number of universes.

Now if the scientists are asked how the universe came about, they have a lot of answers to give. But if they are asked why this evolution took place, then they have no answers. They generally do not explain it as God's creation because they are objective observers who tend only to believe in the material universe. Some say that it happened just by chance. Now that position itself is illogical, because if anything exists by chance then it is tantamount to saying that things do not have any causes. But we see from our everyday lives that everything has a cause: clouds cause rain, wind blows seeds around so that new plants grow. Nothing exists without any reason. If evolution has a cause, then there are two possible explanations. You can accept that the universe was created by God, in which case there will be a lot of contradictions, such as the necessity that suffering and evil must also have been created by God. The other option is to explain that there are infinite numbers of sentient beings whose karmic potentials collectively created this entire universe as an environment for them. The universe we inhabit is created by our own desires and actions. This is why we are here. This, at least, is logical.

At the time of death, we are blown about by the force of our own karmic actions. The result of negative karmic actions is rebirth in the lower realms. In order to discourage ourselves from negative actions, we should try to imagine whether we would be able to bear the sufferings of the lower realms. Having seen that happiness is a consequence of positive actions, we will take great pleasure in accumulating virtue. Equating your own experience with that of others, you will be able to develop strong compassion, for you will understand that their sufferings are no different from your own and they also wish to achieve liberation. It is important to meditate upon the suffering of the animal and hell realms. If we do not make spiritual progress, our negative actions will lead us there. And if we feel we cannot bear the suffering of burning or cold or unquenchable thirst and hunger, then our motivation to practice will increase immeasurably. At the present time, this human existence affords us the opportunity and conditions to rescue ourselves.

The lower forms of existence are rebirth as an animal, hungry ghost, or hell being. According to the scriptures, the hells are located a certain distance directly below Bodh Gaya, the place in India where the Buddha achieved enlightenment. But if you were to actually travel that distance, you would end up in the middle of America. So these teachings should not be taken literally. They were spoken in accordance with the convention of the time, or popular belief. The purpose of the Buddha coming to this world was not to measure the circumference of the world and the distance between the earth and moon, but rather to teach the Dharma, to liberate sentient beings, to relieve sentient beings of their sufferings. If we do not understand the basic approach of Buddhism, we might imagine that the Buddha sometimes spoke in a contradictory and confusing manner. But there is a purpose in each of the diverse philosophical views he taught, and each benefits different types of sentient beings. When he talked about the hells, he must have taken a lot of popular conventions and popular beliefs into account for the specific purpose of causing his listeners to practice the Dharma.

I believe that such states as the various hot and cold hells do exist. If the highest states, like nirvana and omniscience, exist, why should their opposite, the most extreme state of suffering, the most untamed mind, not exist as well? Even within human existence there are different types of people: some enjoy more life and a greater degree of happiness, some have to undergo a greater degree of suffering. Now, all of these differences in experience come about as a result of differences in the causes—actions, or karma. If we go further and compare human beings to the various forms of animal existence, we find that animals' states of mind are more untamed and their suffering and confusion are more obvious. They still have a natural tendency to wish for happiness and avoid suffering. Some animals are very clever: if we try to catch them by giving them some food, they are very cautious. The moment they have eaten, they try to run away, but if we are sincere and patient in giving them food, they can come to trust us completely. Even animals, like dogs and cats, appreciate the value of kindness; they appreciate the value of sincerity and love.

If there are different levels of spiritual attainment based on how tamed the mind has become, there should also be different levels of the untamed mind. Beyond the animal realm are states such as that of hungry ghosts, who cannot satisfy their appetites. Hell realms are states of existence where sufferings are so extreme that the beings there retain hardly any power of judgment or intelligence. The sufferings in the hells are of intense heat and intense cold. Proving that these realms exist is beyond our ordinary logic. But we can conclude that they exist because we know that the Buddha has proven to be so accurate, logical, and consistent on many other important matters, like impermanence and causation, which we can verify logically. Therefore, we can infer that he was correct about the various levels of rebirth as well. The Buddha's motives for explaining the hell realms are only compassion and his desire to teach what would be beneficial to sentient beings for freeing themselves from the cycle of rebirth. Because he has no reason to tell lies, these hidden things must also be true.

Every day we accept as true things that we have no direct way of proving. I was born on July 6, 1935. I know this simply because my mother told me and I believe her. There is no way that I can directly perceive it or logically prove it, but by relying on someone in whom I have confidence and who does not have any reason to tell me lies, I know that I was born on July 6, 1935. Those deeper questions of life after death and the existence of other realms can only be approached by relying on scriptures. We have to prove the validity of those scriptures by applying reason. We cannot just take a quotation at face value. We have to study it and apply it to our lives.

The many different levels of suffering in the lower realms of existence have been explained in different scriptures. Some of the sufferings are so extreme they are beyond our understanding. If you take rebirth in any of these lower realms of existence, how will you be able to bear them? Examine whether you have created the causes and conditions for rebirth in such lower realms of existence. As long as we are under the grip of delusions, the strong forces of hatred and desire, we will be forced against our will to indulge in negative actions that will actually be the cause of our own downfall. If that is the case, then we will have to undergo these sufferings ourselves. If you do not wish to undergo such sufferings or you feel that you would never be able to bear such extreme sufferings, you should restrain your body, speech, and mind from indulging in actions that will accumulate the potential for your fall into such states. Those that have already been accumulated should be properly purified according to the relevant practices. And since everything is impermanent, there is no nonvirtue that cannot be purified.

The more you reflect on these sufferings and the stronger your feeling that they would be unbearable, the more you will see the destructive potential of negative actions. When you meditate on these sufferings, you should try to imagine yourself having taken rebirth in these existences and undergoing the sufferings yourself. It is said, for example, that when reflecting on the sufferings of the hot hells, you should imagine your body burning, or when reflecting on the sufferings of the cold hells, you should think that your body is freezing. The same should be done with regard to the sufferings of animals. It is recommended that you should go to some isolated place and try to simulate the entire experience of such beings, trying to imagine that you are undergoing their suffering yourself. The more powerfully you feel unable to bear the suffering, the greater will be your fear of the lower realms. That leads to knowledge of the destructive power of negative actions and the suffering caused by them. Later, when you meditate on compassion, this practice will help you to increase your compassion toward others who indulge in very grave negative actions. For example, when Tibetans think of the Chinese, whose negative actions consist of genocide, instead of being angered, we try to develop a strong feeling of compassion toward those who are so controlled by their delusions. Although these people may not immediately undergo obvious sufferings, it is only a matter of time, because sooner or later they will have to face the consequences. If we are able to develop a fear of suffering right now as human beings, we have the potential, capacity, and opportunity to prevent the causes for our own downfall. We can purify the negative and accumulate great stores of merit. We will be able to increase the accumulation of merit we already have, and we will be able to dedicate the merit so that it will not be destroyed by anger. If we undertake a proper practice day by day we will be able to make our human lives meaningful.

CHAPTER 6

REFUGE

A Buddhist is someone who, motivated by fear of the sufferings of the cycle of rebirth and of the lower realms of existence,

takes refuge in the Three Jewels: the Buddha, the Dharma (the teachings), and the Sangha (the spiritual community). A Buddhist, through practice and experience, knows that the Three Jewels have the capacity to protect him or her from falling into the lower realms of existence. The eleventh-century teacher Po-to-wa once remarked that when he visited a monastery, even among the senior monks sitting inside in prayer, there were some who were not even Buddhists. Many of them lacked a proper understanding of the Three Jewels. It is taking refuge that fortifies the wish to achieve nirvana.

The Buddha is a being who is totally free of all delusions and faults, who is endowed with all good qualities and has attained the wisdom eliminating the darkness of ignorance. The Dharma is the result of his enlightenment. After having achieved enlightenment, a Buddha teaches, and what he or she teaches, is called the Dharma. The Sangha is made up of those who engage in the practice of the teachings given by the Buddha. These are the basic definitions of the Three Jewels. The activity of the Buddha is to give teachings and show the path. The activity or the function of the Dharma is to eliminate sufferings and their causes, the delusions. The function of the Sangha is to take pleasure in undertaking the practice of this Dharma. You should regard the Buddha with respect. Your attitude toward the Dharma should be one of aspiration, trying to bring about experience of it within your mind, and you should regard the Sangha as noble companions who assist in the process of the path. The Buddha is the master who shows us the path to enlightenment, the Dharma is the actual refuge in which we seek protection from sufferings, and the Sangha consists of spiritual companions through the stages of the path.

One of the benefits of refuge is that all the misdeeds you have committed in the past can be purified, because taking refuge entails accepting the Buddha's guidance and following a path of virtuous action. Most of the negative actions you have committed in the past can be alleviated or reduced and your stores of merit increased. Having sought refuge in the Three Jewels, we will be protected not only from present harm, but also from the harm of rebirth in the lower realms of existence, and the full enlightenment of Buddhahood can be quickly attained. We should never give up the Three Jewels, even at the cost of our lives. There have been many cases in Tibet where the Chinese have tried to force people to abandon their faith. Many responded by saying that they could not give up their faith and have instead chosen to give up their lives. This is the true commitment of taking refuge.

Tsong-kha-pa says that if your fear and conviction are mere words, then taking refuge is just words also, but if your fear and your conviction in the Three Jewels' ability to protect you from such fear are deeply rooted, then your refuge will also be very powerful.

The objects of refuge themselves have achieved a state that is totally free of fear and suffering. If the objects themselves had not obtained such a state, they would not have the ability to protect us, just as someone who has fallen down cannot help you to stand up. Those from whom we seek protection should be free of suffering and fear; otherwise, even though they may have the wish to do so, they will not have the capacity to protect us. The Buddha Shakyamuni is not only free from suffering and fear himself, he is also supremely skillful in leading sentient beings along the right path. This we can understand by reflecting upon the diverse teachings that the Buddha gave to suit the diverse interests and dispositions of sentient beings. He left us with teachings that can reach us no matter what our level of spiritual development. When we realize the importance of this, we will also begin to admire all the religions of the world, because the very aim of their teaching is to help others.

Tsong-kha-pa says that if you reflect upon the great qualities that make something an object of refuge and develop deep, one-pointed conviction in the three objects of refuge, there is no way that you will not be protected. What we need is a deep sense of fear of the sufferings of the lower realms and trust in the capacity of the Three Jewels to protect us from them. We develop this trust through meditating on the qualities of the Buddha, the Dharma, and the Sangha.

The Buddha's compassion is without bias. He does not distinguish between sentient beings who help him and those who do not. His working for the benefit of all the sentient beings is unbiased. These qualifications are complete only in the Buddha, and so he and his many forms and emanations are the refuge, along with the teachings that he has given and the community that emulates him and engages in his way of practice.

The Buddha's speech is such that if he is asked any question or many different questions at the same time, he is said to be able to understand the essence of them all and can reply in one statement. As a result, the answers are in harmony with the questioner's understanding.

The Buddha's wisdom is able to perceive the entire range of phenomena, conventional and absolute, just as if he were looking at something in the palm of his hand. Therefore, all objects of knowledge are perceived and are within the grasp of his wisdom.

The Buddha's mind is also omniscient. The reason that it is possible for a Buddha's mind to perceive the entire sphere of phenomena without exception is that he has achieved a state that is totally free of all obstructions to knowledge. The obstructions to knowledge are the imprints or predispositions left in the mind by the delusions—ignorance of the nature of reality, attachment, and hatred—since beginningless time. When these imprints are removed, we gain the state called omniscience, because there is no longer any obstruction to knowledge. We gain the omniscient state of mind, which perceives the entire range of phenomena without any obstruction.

The Buddha's mind is spontaneously moved by uninterrupted compassion when he sees suffering sentient beings. At the beginning of the path the Buddha developed strong compassion toward all sentient beings and, over the course of the path, has brought that compassion to its ultimate level. Compassion, being a virtuous state of mind and based on the clear nature of the mind, has the potential to increase infinitely.

The body, speech, and mind of the Buddhas are always actively engaged in the task of working for the benefit of others. They fulfill the wishes of sentient beings and lead them through the stages of the path in a skillful manner appropriate to the diverse needs, interests, and dispositions of sentient beings. Tsong-kha-pa says that if your faith in the Buddha is firm, as a result of your recollection of his great kindness and other qualities, your faith in the other two, the Dharma, his teachings, and the Sangha, the spiritual community, will come naturally, and the entire canon of Buddhist scriptures will be like personal advice. So, having developed strong faith in the Buddha, you should develop strong faith in his teachings as well.

Statues or images of a Buddha, irrespective of their material or shape, should never be criticized. You should respect them as you would the Buddha himself. Having taken refuge in the Buddha, you should not be concerned with what the image is made of but should pay it respect regardless. You should never make Buddha statues objects of commerce or use them as collateral for a loan. Once Atisha was asked by one of his disciples to comment on a statue of Manjushri, the Bodhisattva of Wisdom, and said that if Atisha thought it was good, he would like to buy it. Atisha said that one cannot make judgments about the body of Manjushri, but so far as the sculpture was concerned it was quite average, but then he placed the statue on his head as a sign of respect. It seems that when Atisha said the sculpture was quite average, he meant that it did not look very good, so the artist should be more careful. Artists have a very great responsibility to paint images and sculpt statues with a good appearance. Otherwise there is a grave danger of causing many people to accumulate nonvirtuous actions, because sometimes, due to the images' odd appearance, we cannot help laughing.

The method that leads to the omniscient state is the path. The path and the cessation make up the Dharma, the true refuge. The Dharma is something we cannot absorb immediately; it has to be realized through a gradual process. In the context of the practice of refuge, you must be very skillful in being virtuous while avoiding negative actions. That is what is called the practice of the Dharma. If you are afraid of the sufferings of the lower realms of existence, you should transform your mind and prevent it from indulging in negative actions, which cause your downfall. That depends very much upon whether your practice is serious or not, on whether you are committed to accumulating virtuous actions and avoiding negative ones, and that in turn depends upon whether or not you have deep conviction in the law of karma.

There are two different kinds of experience, the desirable and the undesirable, and each has its own cause. Suffering, the undesirable experience, is called the cycle of existence (samsara), and it has its origin in the delusions and the nonvirtuous deeds they compel us to commit. The ultimate form of happiness, the desirable, is nirvana, and it is the result of the practice of the Dharma. The origin of sufferings and of the lower realms of existence is the ten negative actions [described in chapter 7]. The desired prosperity and rebirth in favorable realms of existence are caused by the observance of pure morality, or the practice of the ten virtuous actions. In order to prevent your taking rebirth in the lower realms of existence and undergoing suffering there, you must put a stop to their causes by turning your body, speech, and mind toward virtuous actions. The degree of your commitment to serious practice depends very much upon how convinced you are, how deep your conviction is in the law of cause and effect, how fully you believe that undesirable sufferings and misfortunes are the consequences of negative actions, and how convinced you are that desirable consequences, like happiness, pleasure, and prosperity, are the results of positive actions. It is very important first of all, therefore, to develop a deep conviction in the infallibility of the law of karma.

Having taken refuge in the Dharma, as a commitment of affirmation, one should show respect to Buddhist texts. You should not step over even a single page, and the texts should be kept in a clean place. You should not have a possessive attitude toward scriptures; you should not sell them or place them as security for borrowing money. You should not place your eyeglasses or pens on top of the scriptures. When you turn the page, you should not lick your finger. It is said that Geshe Chen-nga-wa used to stand up when he saw texts being carried by, but later when due to his age he was unable to stand up, he used to still fold his hands. When Atisha was in western Tibet there was a tantric practitioner who would not take teachings from him. One day Atisha saw another Tibetan mark the place in a text he was reading by picking some food from his teeth. Atisha asked him not to do that, and as a result the tantric practitioner saw Atisha's commitment to the precepts for taking refuge, was very impressed, and is said to have become his disciple.

We should also have faith in the Sangha, the spiritual community. When we talk of the Sangha, it chiefly refers to those superior beings who, as a result of their diligent practice, have realized the Dharma within their own minds and penetrated the nature of reality. The real Sangha is those who are always engaged in the practice of the Dharma, who uphold the precepts properly, who are excellent in their observance of morality, and who are always truthful, honest, pure in heart, and always filled with compassion.

Having taken refuge in the Sangha, you should never insult any monk or nun who maintains the ordained life. You should be respectful of them. Within the Sangha community you should not be sectarian or hold any rivalry. In places like Thailand, the Sangha is held in great respect. Just as people respect them, so the monks also should not behave disgracefully, causing the laypeople to lose faith. In general, I do not think it is necessarily good to have a large community of monks, as there was in Tibet, but that it is better to have truly pure monks, even if it is only a small community. Whether you become a monk or not is a matter of personal choice, but after having chosen to lead the life of a monk or nun, it is naturally better not to be a disgrace to the doctrine. Otherwise, not only is it bad for you, it also causes other people to lose their faith and unnecessarily accumulate nonvirtues. It is said that Drom-ton-pa would not even step over a small piece of red or yellow cloth, because it represented the robes of monks and nuns.

Tsong-kha-pa says that taking refuge is really the entrance to the Buddhist community, and if our refuge is more than mere words and is really deeply felt, we will be invulnerable to harms from human beings and will make easy progress in our practice. Realizing these benefits, we should try to reinforce our fear of suffering and develop a strong faith and conviction in the Three Jewels' capacity to protect us from those sufferings. We should try to make our practice of refuge as powerful as possible and try never to act against the precepts that we have taken. Thus, with awareness of death and fear of the lower realms of existence, we will find that the Three Jewels have the capacity to protect us, that they are a true source of refuge.

The Buddha is the master who reveals the actual refuge, and the Sangha is like the companions on the path leading to enlightenment. The actual refuge is the Dharma, because through the realization of the Dharma, we will become free and be relieved from suffering. The Dharma consists of cessation and the path to cessation. The absence of or freedom from delusions is called cessation. If we do not apply the appropriate antidote to our faults and delusions, they continue to arise. But after the application of the antidote, once a delusion is totally uprooted, it will never arise again. Such a state, free from delusions or the stains of the mind, is said to be a cessation. In short, anything that we want to abandon, like suffering and its origin, can be eliminated by the application of opponent forces.

The final cessation, also known as nirvana, is a state of complete liberation.

The Buddhas, the fully enlightened ones, are inconceivable, and the Dharma, their teaching, is inconceivable, and the Sangha is also inconceivable. Therefore, if you develop inconceivable faith, the result will also be inconceivable. It is said in the scriptures that if the benefits of taking refuge in the Three Jewels could be made visible, the entire universe would be too small to enclose it, just as the great oceans cannot be measured in your hands. Being mindful of these great benefits, you should rejoice in the opportunity to make offerings to the Three Jewels and take refuge in them. You will be able to alleviate the influences of negative actions committed in addition to karmic obstructions. All these will be eliminated, and you will be counted as a sublime being, which will please the Three Jewels.

CHAPTER 7

KARMA

The consequences of karma are definite:
negative actions always bring about
suffering, and positive actions always bring

happiness. If you do good, you will have happiness; if you do bad, you yourself will suffer. Our karmic actions follow us from lifetime to lifetime, which explains why some people who indulge constantly in negativity are still successful on the worldly level or why others who are committed to spiritual practice face myriad difficulties. Karmic actions have been committed in infinite numbers of lives, so there is infinite potential for an infinite number of outcomes.

The potential of karma always increases over time. Small seeds have the potential to produce massive fruits. That is also true of the inner cause and effect; even a small action can bring about a massive consequence, whether positive or negative. For example, a small boy once offered the Buddha a handful of sand, vividly imagining it to be gold. In a future life, the boy was reborn as the great Buddhist emperor, Ashoka. From the slightest positive action can come the greatest consequence of happiness, and in the same way the smallest negative action can bring about very intense suffering. The potential of karma to increase within our mindstreams is far greater than the potential of mere physical causes, such as an apple seed. Just as drops of water can fill a large vessel, in the same way the smallest actions, when continuously committed, can fill the minds of sentient beings.

Within the human community we see a lot of differences. Some people are always successful in their lives, some are always unsuccessful, some are happy, some have a good presence and calmness of mind. Some people seem always to face great misfortune, against our expectations. Some people whom you would expect to have misfortune do not. All of this testifies to the fact that not everything is within our hands. Sometimes, when we try to start an endeavor, we accumulate all the necessary conditions that are required for its success, but still something is missing. We say that someone is lucky and someone is unlucky, but this alone is not enough; luck must have a reason, a cause. According to the Buddhist explanation, it is the consequence of your actions committed either in the past life or in the earlier part of this life. When the potential has ripened, then even if you are facing adverse circumstances, still the endeavor proves successful. But in some cases, even if you have all the necessary conditions gathered, still you fail.

We Tibetans have become refugees and have undergone a lot of suffering, but still we are relatively fortunate and successful. In Tibet the Chinese have tried to make the entire population equal by creating communes and limiting private property. But still, in the communes, some gardens grow more vegetables than others, and some cows give more milk. This shows that there is a great difference between the merits of individuals. If someone's virtuous actions ripen, even though the authorities confiscate his or her wealth, this person will still prove successful because of the force of his or her merit, because of the force of that karma. If you accumulate virtuous actions properly, such as avoiding killing, freeing animals, and cultivating patience toward others, it will be beneficial in the future and in the lives to come, whereas if you indulge in negative actions continuously, you definitely will face the consequences in the future. If you do not believe in the principle of karma, then you can do as you like.

Once you commit an action, the cause for a reaction remains and increases until its effect is experienced. If you have not committed the action you will never face the consequences; once you have committed the action, unless you purify it through proper practices, or if it is a virtuous action, unless it is destroyed by anger or opposing factors, the effect of the action will be experienced. An action, even if it was performed many lifetimes ago, will never lose its effect simply due to the passage of time.

Positive and negative actions are determined by one's own motivation. If the motivation is good, all actions become positive; if the motivation is wrong, all actions become negative. The karmic actions are of many different types; some are totally virtuous, some are totally nonvirtuous, some are mixed. If the motivation is right, although the action itself might appear quite violent, it will bring about happiness, whereas if the motivation is wrong and devious, then even though the action might seem beneficial and positive, in reality it will be a negative action. It all depends upon the mind: if your mind is tamed and trained, all actions become positive, whereas if your mind is not tamed and it is influenced constantly by desire and hatred, although actions might appear to be positive, in reality you will accumulate negative karma. If more people believed in the law of karma, we would likely never have to have a police force or a penal system. But if individuals lack this internal faith in karmic actions, even though externally the people might apply all sorts of techniques to execute the law, they will not be able to bring about a peaceful society. In this modern world sophisticated equipment is used for surveillance and for detecting lawbreakers. But the more fascinating and sophisticated these machines are, the more sophisticated and determined criminals become. If this human society is to change for the better, then enforcing a law externally alone will not be enough; we need some kind of internal deterrent.

A civilized, peaceful, way of life and a spiritually based morality should go hand in hand. Before the Chinese invaded in 1959, the kings of Tibet created laws for the country based on the Buddhist concept of morality. People throughout the world say that the

Tibetan people are exceptionally gentle and benevolent. I do not see any other reason to explain this unique feature of our culture than by the fact that it has been based on the Buddhist teaching of nonviolence for so many centuries.

There are three doors through which we commit actions: body, speech, and mind. Through these doors, we can commit either the ten positive deeds or the ten nonvirtuous deeds. Of the nonvirtuous deeds, three are physical, four are verbal, and three are mental. The first physical nonvirtue is taking the life of another. For killing to take place, there must be another living being; taking one's own life is not regarded in the same way because no other person is involved. If you have the initial motive of killing a certain person, but in the actual performance of the killing you happen to kill someone else by mistake, then it does not constitute a complete nonvirtuous action of killing. On the other hand, when your primary motive is to kill anyone you meet, then if you kill anyone, that constitutes accumulation of the full nonvirtue of killing.

Killing can be motivated by any of the three poisons: attachment, hatred, or ignorance. For example, we can kill animals out of attachment for the meat, we can kill enemies out of hatred, and we can perform animal sacrifices out of ignorance. Whether you do the deed yourself or you let others do it for you does not matter; both constitute the same negative action of killing. In order for the action of killing to be complete, the person who is killed must die prior to the killer.

The second negative action is stealing. Stealing can be motivated by attachment, or you can steal out of hatred for someone, in order to harm that person. Stealing could also be motivated by ignorance due to a mistaken belief that you can take anything you want. The intention is to separate the possession from its owner. Stealing can be done by force or by stealth, or you can borrow something and let the owner forget and then keep it yourself, or you borrow money and do not pay it back. The deed is complete when you think that the object now belongs to you. Even if you do not do it yourself directly, if you let others do it for you, it still constitutes stealing.

The last of the three negative actions of the body is sexual misconduct, which is a sexual act performed with an unsuitable person, with an unsuitable part of the body, at an unsuitable time, in an unsuitable place, or against the will of the other person—which of course includes rape. For a man, unsuitable women include one's own mother, the wife or girlfriend of someone else, prostitutes temporarily paid by someone else, one's relatives, or ordained women, like nuns. It also includes other males. Unsuitable parts of the body are the anus and the mouth. Unsuitable places are around the residence of one's own spiritual master or near a stupa or inside a temple or in the presence of one's own parents. Unsuitable time for a man is when the woman is having menstruation, when she is pregnant, and when she is suffering from an illness that intercourse would worsen. If a man engages in sexual intercourse in these ways, even with his own wife, it is said to be sexual misconduct. Generally speaking, intercourse is engaged in out of attachment, but one could also do so out of hatred, such as a man sleeping with the wife of an enemy. It is also sometimes done out of ignorance, thinking that through sexual intercourse one can gain great realizations. The negative action of sexual misconduct can only be committed by oneself, and the act is made definite when the two sexual organs meet.

The next four negative actions are deeds of speech. The first is telling lies. This includes speaking contrary to what one has seen, heard, or knows to be fact. Lying can be motivated by attachment, hatred, or ignorance. The intention is to confuse the other person, and it can be carried out either by speaking or nodding the head and gesturing with a hand. Any action done out of the intention to confuse someone constitutes the negative action of lying. If the other person hears it, that constitutes completion of this act.

Next is divisive talk. The intention is to cause dissension between friends or people in the spiritual community for one's own sake or for the sake of others. Whether one succeeds in causing dissension or not, the moment the other person hears the divisive talk, that constitutes the completion of this act.

Next is verbal abuse. The intention is to speak harshly, and the deed is complete when the abusive words are heard by the person to whom they are directed. Abuse includes insulting others, speaking about their faults, whether true or untrue; if one does it to hurt the other person, it is abuse.

Next is senseless gossip. It is frivolousness without any purpose, and it can be motivated by any of the three poisons. One's intention is simply to chat without any reason, to just gossip without any purpose. The execution of this act does not require a second person. You do not need a partner; you can do this by talking to yourself. Idle gossip would include talking about wars, the faults of others, or arguing just for the sake of argument. This would also include reading unimportant books out of attachment.

Lastly, there are three negative actions of the mind, the first being covetousness. The object of covetousness is possessions belonging to others. The delusion that prompts covetousness can be any of the three poisons—desire, hatred, or ignorance. Completing this nonvirtue involves five factors: strong attachment toward others' possessions, the desire to hoard wealth, coveting another's possessions, desiring another's possessions for oneself, and not seeing the harm in coveting others' belongings. If these five factors are complete, then when one covets something, it completes the execution of this mental act.

Next is harmful intent, which is similar to harsh speech. The intention is to hurt someone or speak harshly or hope that others will suffer misfortune and fail in their activities. Once one indulges in such thoughts, the outcome or completion is either that you physically strike the person or mentally intend to do so. This would also require five factors: that one has as the basic motive hatred or anger, that one has a lack of patience, that one does not realize the faults of anger, that one actually intends to harm the other person, and that one does not realize the faults of the harmful intent sufficiently to overwhelm one's harmful intention. Simply wishing that the other person would suffer is harmful intent.

The last of the ten negative actions is wrong views or perverse views in which one denies the existence of things that exist. There are generally four types of wrong views: wrong views with respect to cause, with respect to effect, with respect to the function of a thing, and with respect to the existence of a thing. Wrong view with respect to cause would be believing that there is no karmic action; with respect to effect would be believing that certain actions do not have consequences; with respect to function would be thinking that children are not raised by their parents and seeds do not produce their results, and also thinking that there is no past life or life after death. The fourth type of wrong view is wrong view with respect to existent things—believing out of ignorance and attachment that enlightened beings, nirvana, and the Three Jewels do not exist. Tsong-kha-pa says that although there are many different types of wrong views, these wrong views really cut the root of one's collection of virtue and as a result force the individual to indulge in negative actions without any control. Therefore, wrong views about the Three Jewels and the law of cause and effect are said to be the greatest of wrong views.

We should also be aware of the relative gravity of karmic actions. When the deed is motivated by very strong delusions, then the deed is said to be very grave. The way in which the deed is actually performed also determines the karmic weight. For example, if a murder is committed with great pleasure, first torturing the person and then mocking and insulting the person, it is said to be very grave because of the inhuman manner in which that person or living being was killed. If the murderer's mind has no conscience or sense of shame, then because he or she lacks the opponent forces, the negative action of killing is very grave. If your killing of a living being is motivated by ignorance, like making a sacrificial offering, thinking this killing is actually a religious act and it does not constitute a negative action, then that is said to be very grave.

In general, the more you perform certain negative actions, the more grave the act becomes. The weight of the karma also depends on the person who performs the action. If you dedicate your merit for the benefit of other sentient beings for the purpose of achieving enlightenment, it is said to be more powerful, whereas if it is dedicated to lesser aims it is said to be less powerful. This applies to negative action as well; the more forceful the motivating delusions are, the more forceful the karmic action is, and among all these delusions anger is said to be the most powerful. A single moment of anger directed toward a bodhisattva would destroy all the virtuous collections that you might have accumulated over the last thousand eons.

The effect of negative actions is based also on the intensity of the delusions that prompt them. There are also effects that correspond to the cause. For example, as a result of killing, even when after taking rebirth in the lower realms of existence one takes rebirth as a human being, one's life will be short. As a result of stealing one will lack material wealth, as a result of sexual misconduct one will have a very unfaithful spouse, as a result of harsh speech people will insult you, as a result of divisive speech there will be dissension among one's friends, and so forth. Another type of effect is instinctive behavior. As a result of killing in a past life, even as a human being one would have instinctive impulses, taking delight in killing. There are also environmental effects, which ripen more collectively for a community. As a result of killing, for example, one would have to live in a place where the crops are not very good, harvests are not abundant, the countryside is very desolate, the climate is not very good, full of poisonous trees and thorns. As an environmental effect of stealing, a farmer would not have successful crops. As an environmental effect of wrong views, one would lack protection and one would have no refuge.

If as a result of morality one refrains from indulging in these negative actions and resolves not to indulge in them, that constitutes accumulation of positive actions. If one does not have the ability or the capacity to indulge in negative actions, however, that does not mean that you have accumulated virtuous actions; virtuous actions can be accumulated only when one has the ability and capacity to do these negative actions but one does not do so out of moral restraint.

Some actions are committed but not done intentionally, like accidental killings, killing in dreams, or doing something against one's will. In these cases the action is committed but the karma is not accumulated; the completion of the karmic action does not take place, because it lacks the necessary factor of intention. If, on the other hand, you compel someone to commit a nonvirtuous act on your behalf, then the negative karma is accumulated by you.

The result of an action can ripen within this lifetime or within the very next life or after an interval of many lives. Some of the actions that are very grave, done out of ignorance or intense hatred, are said to be so grave that they will produce their results even in this lifetime. That also is the case with some positive actions; if you have strong compassion for sentient beings, if you have strong refuge in the Three Jewels, and if you repay the kindness of the spiritual master and your parents, the fruits of these actions are said to be so powerful that they will begin to ripen within this lifetime.

Attaining a human form is mainly the result of observing pure morality and refraining from the ten negative actions. However, in order to attain a human form that is endowed with the conditions that will expedite one's process on the path, other factors are necessary. These include a long life for the completion of Dharma practice. It also helps to have a sound, handsome, and healthy body as well as birth in a respectable family, because then you would naturally command great respect from people and you would have greater influence. Other factors that are mentioned in the texts are having credible speech and a powerful body and mind so that you would not be vulnerable to interferences. With an attractive form the mere sight of you will attract disciples and cause them to have great faith in you, without any difficulty. Coming from a respected family, people will listen to you and heed your advice. You will be able to gather many people together under your influence by giving them material aid, and you will cause others to take what you say as true because of your credible speech. Whatever you say will be accomplished quickly, as you wished, just as when a king gives an order. You will not be afraid or shy to teach the Dharma to a large crowd of people, and there will be fewer obstacles to the practice of the Dharma. By having a powerful body and mind you will be able to endure great physical hardship, and you will not have any regrets or frustration about working to fulfill any of your own or others' aims.

Each of these various qualities has a specific karmic cause. The cause of a long life is always having a helpful, altruistic attitude, never harming others. The cause of a strong, healthy body is giving others new clothes and abstaining from losing your temper. Birth in a re-spected family is the result of always being humble, never being proud, and regarding oneself as a servant to one's teacher and parents. The cause of great wealth is giving material aid to poor people, and the cause of credible speech is abstaining from negative actions of speech. Having great influence is the result of making offerings to the Three Jewels, one's own parents, teach-ers, and so on. Having a powerful body and mind is the result of giving food and drink to others. If you ac-cumulate these causes, you will achieve the unique human existence with those qualities.

If we remain idle and do not think seriously about karmic law, we might sometimes feel that we are not accumulating any negative actions and that we are good practitioners. If we analyze our thoughts and ac-tions closely, however, we will find that we are engag-ing in idle speech, harming others, or engaging in cov-etousness on a daily basis. We will find that we actually lack the primary factor of deep conviction that is nec-essary to really observe the law of karma. We need to see the gap between the practice of the Dharma and the way we are living our lives at the moment. In order to close the gap, integrate the knowledge of the law of cause and effect into your actions. If you see the poten-tial danger of your way of thinking and acting, then you will repeatedly cultivate the resolve to correct your thoughts and behavior.

Tsong-kha-pa says that although we should make great effort not to indulge in these negative actions ever again, as a result of long association with delusions, we sometimes find ourselves uncontrollably having committed them. These should not be left unheeded. Rather, we should engage in the purification techniques that the Buddha himself has recommended. He said that by applying four opponent powers we will be able to purify the negativity that has already been committed and will be able to overcome it. The first is the power of regret. By reflecting upon the gravity of the consequences of negative actions, you should from the depths of your heart develop a deep sense of regret for the actions committed. The second is the power of purification. This can be achieved through a variety of techniques, including reciting, memorizing, and reading sutras, meditating on emptiness, reciting mantras, making images of the Buddha, making offerings, and reciting the names of the Buddhas. These purification practices should be undertaken until you see signs and indications of success in your purification practice. These signs include having dreams of vomiting, dreams of drinking milk or curd, seeing the sun and moon in a dream, dreaming of flying or of fires burning or of overpowering buffaloes or people with black coats, dreaming about monks and nuns, dreaming about climbing hills, and dreaming of listening to teachings. These are indications of success in your purification practice.

The third is the power of resolve not to engage in the nonvirtuous deed in the future. If you have the power of resolve and restrain yourself from committing the ten negative actions, you will not only be able to purify the negativities of the ten nonvirtuous actions alone, but you also will have the power to purify the delusions and the imprints left by them. If your power of resolve is very superficial, your purification practice will also be superficial. The last power is meditation on taking refuge in the Buddha, Dharma, and Sangha and developing the wish to become enlightened for the sake of all sentient beings.

If a negative action is committed and left unpurified, it will have the potential to bring about rebirth in the lower realms of existence. Negative actions can either be totally purified in the sense that their potential will be totally destroyed, or their potential to produce rebirth in lower realms will be destroyed but they could manifest as simple headaches within this lifetime. That is, any negative actions that would otherwise have brought about their consequences over a long time can be experienced within a short period of time. These results depend upon whether or not the practitioner is skillful in the purification practice, whether or not the four powers are complete, and also how intense one's practice is and for how long this purification practice is undertaken. In some cases the potential of karmic action is destroyed; in other cases it can manifest in lighter experiences. You should not take this as contradictory to the statement in the scriptures that karmic actions once committed will never lose their potential even for a hundred eons. This means that if the karmic actions once committed are left unpurified, then they will never lose their potential just because of the passage of time. There is no action that cannot be purified. Purification destroys the potential of the negative karmic actions in the same way in which positive actions lose their potential due to the arising of anger. But the Buddha has said that you can never purify a karmic action once it has already produced its results. For example, the negative experiences we have had in this life are effects of negative actions committed in the past—actions that have already taken place; there is no way you can purify these.

Tsong-kha-pa says that since it is possible for positive actions to lose their potential by the arising of their opposing factors, like anger, we should not only be very careful to accumulate virtue, we should also be equally careful to protect virtues after having once accumulated them. This is done by dedicating our merit for the achievement of enlightenment for the purpose of achieving Buddhahood. It is said that once you have dedicated your merit for the achievement of such aims, then until you fulfill that aim, the virtuous action you have accumulated will never lose its potential. It is like depositing your money in a bank impregnable to robbers—who in this case would be anger, attachment, or ignorance.

Although through the application of proper opponent forces we can purify the negativities totally and destroy their potential to bring about undesirable consequences, it is far better simply not to commit these negative actions in the first place. Therefore, it is better right from the beginning never to indulge in them, never to stain your mind with such negative actions. Tsong-kha-pa says it is analogous to someone breaking a leg; later it is healed, but compared to a leg that has never been broken, it is far different.

Some might think that since in other scriptures the prosperity and benefits of this life within samsara are described as objects to be avoided and renounced, it is not suitable for a practitioner to wish to gain favorable forms of existence, because that also is a life within samsara. This is a very wrong attitude. When we talk of aims, they are of two types: temporary aims and ultimate aims. Temporary aims include achieving the precious human form in the next life. On the basis of such a precious human form you would be able to carry on your practice of the Dharma in order that you can eventually fulfill your ultimate aim of achieving enlightenment. Although for a Mahayana practitioner the ultimate aim is to work for the achievement of omniscience for the sake of other sentient beings, it is also necessary for a practitioner to wish to gain a favorable rebirth in the future, like human existence, so that he or she will be able to continue practicing. Shantideva says that the precious human life should be thought of as a vessel in which one can cross over the ocean of samsara. In order to fulfill the ultimate aim of achieving the omniscient state, you must attain the precious human form in many lifetimes. The basic cause of achieving such favorable forms of rebirth is the practice of morality.

After having developed the wish to undertake the practice of the Dharma, it is very difficult for the majority of people totally to renounce the world. The best type of practitioner renounces worldly life and spends the rest of his or her life in an isolated, solitary practice. This is really commendable and it has great benefits, but for the majority of us it is very difficult to undertake a practice like that. You have to also think of your own life and also work within the community and serve the people. You should not be totally preoccupied with worldly activities; you should also expend much energy and time for the practice of the Dharma aimed at the betterment of your future life. You begin to realize that compared to your future destiny, the affairs of this life are not that important.

By taking refuge and living within the karmic law, making effort to abandon negative actions and accumulate positive actions, you might enjoy a favorable rebirth in the future. However, we should not be satisfied with that alone, because that favorable rebirth, as a place in samsara, is of the nature of suffering. We rather should cultivate the perception that every form of existence within this cycle of existence is of the nature of suffering. Since beginningless time, we have had this instinctive attachment to the prosperity of samsara, and we have never been able to perceive the pleasures of samsara for what they are: actual and genuine sufferings. As long as prisoners do not know that they are in prison and do not perceive the life of the prisoner as difficult and painful to bear, they will not develop any genuine wish to free themselves from prison. The same is true of samsara: as long as you are not able to perceive the defects of life within this cycle of existence, you will never develop a genuine wish to gain nirvana, freedom from samsara.

You should not have the wrong notion that Buddhism is pessimistic. Rather, it is very optimistic, because the aim of each individual is complete enlightenment, which brings a total, lasting happiness. Buddhism reminds us that this is possible for everyone. The pleasures of samsara seem desirable temporarily, but they can never satisfy us no matter how long we enjoy them, and they are not reliable because they are subject to change. In contrast to the bliss and happiness of nirvana, which is ultimate, permanent, and eternal, these pleasures and happiness within samsara become insignificant.

CHAPTER 8

THE FOUR TRUTHS

In order to build a solid aspiration for liberation from the cycle of existence, we must thoroughly examine our condition

and consider the reasons for wanting to escape. The first thing to recognize is that our bodies and minds are predisposed to suffering. The Four Noble Truths—the Buddha's first teaching—address this issue directly. These truths are the truth of suffering, the truth of the origin of suffering, the truth of the cessation of suffering, and the truth of the path leading to cessation. The Buddha's decision to teach the truths in this sequence has great significance for our practice. In order to underline the importance of understanding that what we ordinarily regard as happiness is in fact suffering, the Buddha taught the truth of suffering first.

When you perceive that you have fallen into an ocean of suffering, you will develop the wish to be liberated from that suffering, and for that purpose you will see first that it is necessary to eliminate the origin of suffering. When you look for the origin of suffering, you find the delusions and karmic actions. You will then be able to perceive that the cycle of existence and its sufferings are produced by your own karmic actions, which in turn are propelled by the delusions, which are rooted in the mistaken belief in the solidity, or inherent existence, of the self. If we analyze how we think of the self, we will find that we tend to think of it as existing intrinsically, independent of the mind and body. And yet when we seek to locate it, it eludes us. The Buddha taught that no such self exists and that our belief in an independent self is the root cause of all suffering.

Among the many different religions, one group does not accept any life after death and one group does. Those who accept life after death may be divided into two groups: one asserts that the delusions and stains of the mind can be eliminated and purified, while the other believes that they cannot. The latter group maintains that as long as the mind is there, we can never purify and separate the mind from its delusions. Therefore, elimination of delusion means that the mind itself must be terminated. Within the group that believes that the mind can be eventually separated from its stains and delusions—that is, who believe in nirvana— one group identifies nirvana with a kind of a place that is totally free of sufferings, a pleasant place up in a lofty realm. Others identify nirvana with the state of mind in which the delusions are totally dissolved into reality.

Nirvana exists on the very basis of the mind itself. This is the Buddhist view.

The Truth of Suffering

In order to understand the first truth, that of suffering, one must meditate on suffering. We see ourselves as the most precious thing in the universe, and we treat ourselves as though we are more precious than a Buddha. But that kind of clinging has still not led to perfect happiness. Since beginningless time we have gone through the cycle of existence and had an infinite number of lives. From childhood till now, we have gone through ups and downs, all kinds of frustrations and confusions. Our lives are beset by problems, sufferings, miseries, frustrations. Eventually this life will end with death, and after that we have no certainty where it will lead us. We should really examine whether there is a way to free ourselves from this unsatisfactory existence. If life were such that it arose independent of causes and conditions and ended without further continuity, we would be helpless to escape. And if that were true, we should live by hedonistic principles. But we know that suffering is something we really do not desire and that if it is possible to obtain total freedom from it, that this freedom is worth achieving.

Karmic actions of body, speech, and mind are what bind us to the cycle of existence and suffering. As we know, we can accumulate these actions even within a moment, and that moment can throw us into a lower realm. This bondage is rooted in the untamed mind and caused by our own ignorance, our own misunderstanding of the self. This instinctive notion of a kind of independent, isolated self prompts us to indulge in all sorts of negative actions, which result in suffering. This self-centered attitude has long been our master; we have always obeyed its order. We should realize that we have not benefited from following its advice. As long as we do so there is no chance for happiness. At this juncture we should examine whether or not it is possible to overcome this delusion.

The very experience of birth is painful for both mother and child. After we are born, delusion has an instinctive hold over our bodies and minds, preventing the mind from being directed toward practice of the Dharma. Our own bodies become causes for the arising of delusions. For example, when the body is weakened by certain diseases you get angry, and when it is healthier you have attachment. Birth is inevitably followed by death, and death is followed by another rebirth. If this were not enough, rebirth itself serves as the basis for further sufferings, because this rebirth provides the setting for further delusions, which again motivate negative actions that have karmic consequences.

This human existence, which we hold as precious, arose from something filthy. Our bodies are produced by the combination of the regenerative fluids of the parents, the semen and ovum. If we find blood and semen on a cloth or a drop spilled on the ground, we are repulsed. Yet we continue to worship our own bodies. We try to cover our bodies with fine clothes and disguise the smell with perfume. Our parents also arose from the same substances, as did their parents and grandparents. If we trace it back, we will see that the body is the end product of all these impure substances. If we take it one more step, we can see that the body is like a machine for producing excrement and urine. When you see earthworms that eat mud at one end and then excrete it from the other, it is really very pitiful. The same is true of our own bodies; we keep on eating and we keep on excreting. Such a body is nothing to cherish.

In addition, human beings have the potential to threaten the very survival of the earth. As a result of their untamed minds, people like Stalin, Hitler, and Mao not only have accumulated limitless stores of negative actions, but also they have affected the lives of innumerable persons, causing distress, suffering, and torment.

Then there is the suffering of aging. Aging comes about gradually; otherwise we would not be able to bear it at all. When we become old, we lose the suppleness we had when we were young; we cannot digest the food we once enjoyed. We are unable to recall the names of people or things that we used to remember vividly. Gradually our teeth fall out, our hair falls out, and we lose our eyesight and hearing. Eventually we reach a stage of decline at which people begin to find the mere sight of us repulsive. When you have reached a stage when you need the assistance of others, people will shy away from you.

Next, there is the suffering of illness. Physical suffering and mental anxiety increase, and you have to spend days and nights wracked by illness. Sickness prevents you from eating the food that you really like, and you are prevented from doing the things that you love to do. You have to take medicines that taste awful. Next is the suffering of death. You will part from your precious belongings, and you will part from your own loved ones, and you will part from your own physical body that has accompanied you throughout your life. The suffering of death is very obvious to us; there is no need to explain it further.

Then there is the suffering of meeting with the unwanted, such as enemies. Within this lifetime, many experiences take place against our wishes. We Tibetans have lost our freedom; this is the suffering of meeting with the unwanted. Even people in a superpower like the United States are beset with all sorts of problems. Since they have been brought up in such material affluence, sometimes they get spoiled. As a result of unbridled competition they live with more anxiety than others. Competition is good to a point, but if it gets out of control, as it has in the United States, it creates jealousy and overwhelming dissatisfaction. In the materially developed countries, there is so much food that people sometimes throw it into the ocean, but on the other side of the planet are countries, such as those in Africa, where millions of people are starving. It is difficult to find someone who is completely satisfied.

Next is the suffering of having what we want taken away from us. We Tibetans lost our country and had to part from our loved ones. There is also the suffering of not obtaining what is desired although it is sought. Even though you work in the fields, you do not get a good harvest, or if you start a business, it is not successful.

Another perspective on suffering is to contemplate the suffering of uncertainty. In this cycle of existence, over the course of many rebirths, and sometimes within a single lifetime, everything changes. Our parents will turn into enemies, our relatives will turn into enemies, our enemies will turn into friends, our parents will be born later as our own children. There is no certainty. Tsong-kha-pa says that we should try to prevent the kind of emotional fluctuations that we have toward other people, based on the discrimination or classification of some as enemies and some as relatives or friends. We should reflect upon the uncertainty of the entire life within this cycle of existence and try to develop some sense of aversion for samsara.

There is also the suffering of lack of contentment. If we really consider how much food we have eaten over the course of one life, then we feel depressed and wonder what use we have made of it. If that is the case with this lifetime, what if we consider all of our past lifetimes—the amount of milk we have drunk from our mothers as children, for example? It is beyond our imagination. You should reflect upon all sorts of prosperity and suffering in this cycle of existence and think that there is no kind of experience that you have not already undergone in samsara. We try to enjoy ourselves in order to have some kind of mental satisfaction, but the pleasure and happiness of samsara are such that no matter how much we try to enjoy them, there is no sense of contentment; it is just endless. You should reflect upon this lack of contentment, which in itself is a great suffering. We have gone through all these experiences and ups and downs in samsara infinite numbers of times. Reflecting upon the pointlessness of such experiences, you should determine that if you do not put a stop to this vicious circle now, there is no point in going on at all. Thus we should develop a deep sense of aversion toward the entire range of experience within this cycle of existence.

There is the suffering of having to discard the body again and again. Up to now we have lived so many lives and had so many bodies, and still we have not been able to make use of them in a meaningful way. We have achieved nothing simply by taking on these countless bodies. We have had to undergo conception again and again. The Buddha said that if we were to count our mothers by setting aside pebbles, with each one representing our mother, there would be no end to this counting.

Reflect upon the fact that all the prosperity within samsara ends in some kind of misery and frustration. As the texts say, the end of gathering is depletion, the end of high status is downfall, the end of meeting is separation, and the end of living is death. In short, all experiences, pleasure, and happiness within this cycle of existence, no matter how forceful and how great they appear, end with misery.

Finally, a further perspective is provided by the three types of sufferings. The first type is called the suffering of suffering, the obvious experiences of physical and mental pain that we ordinarily identify as suffering. The second type is called the suffering of change. Because all worldly pleasures and happiness eventually turn into sufferings, they are called sufferings of change. Sufferings of change are misidentified as experiences of happiness. For example, if you have a fever or you feel very hot and cool water is thrown on your body, you feel a kind of pleasure. This is what we regard as happiness. Or if you have been walking for a long time and after a while you get a chance to sit down, at that moment it seems really very blissful. However, in actual fact it is not a blissful experience; what you are actually experiencing is a gradual cessation of the earlier suffering. If sitting down were a true pleasure, then going on sitting should cause you the same pleasure, but if you continue sitting, after a while you will get tired and will want to stand up.

The third type of suffering is the suffering of pervasive conditioning, the fact that our minds and bodies are so conditioned as to be capable of undergoing suffering at any moment. The three types of suffering can be illustrated in this way. If you have a burn and you apply an ointment that gives you some kind of feeling of protection and pleasure, that is like the suffering of change, because although that is momentarily pleasurable, the pleasure will not last. Then if someone touches it accidentally or hot water is splashed on it, you really feel acute pain. That is obvious suffering, the suffering of suffering. What makes these two sufferings possible is that we have that burn in the first place. If we had not been burned, we would not have the subsequent experiences. The burn provides the condition for further suffering, just as our possession of a body and mind predisposes us to further suffering. And the nature of the body itself provides the condition to be burned. It is predisposed to suffering. This is the suffering of pervasive conditioning.

We should recognize that the sufferings of animals, hungry ghosts, and hell beings can also occur among humans. In Tibet many people died of starvation after the Chinese occupation began. It seems that they sometimes had to eat the leaves of trees and also some insects and worms. These are very similar to the experiences of hungry ghosts. The same suffering is occurring now in Africa, where millions of people are starving because of famine. When countries are at war, due to political differences, the people suffer almost as they do in the hell realms. When Stalin came to power, he ruled the Soviet Union in an authoritarian and inhuman way. It is said that before the Second World War, 14.5 million people lost their lives under Stalin's rule. They were Russian peasants, many of whom died of starvation or torture. The Communist party members had access to good food and a good life. When they had lunch they had to be protected by guards because of the danger that the peasants might riot and take the food.

Even the gods suffer. They are able to foresee their deaths before they die, so they suffer mentally. It is said that their flower garlands wilt and their clothes and bodies begin to stink. After having experienced all the pleasures of heaven, they have exhausted the entire potential of their positive actions. As a result, when they die they will go straight to the lower realms of existence. Tsong-kha-pa says that having thus reflected upon the general sufferings of all of samsara in general and also the specific sufferings of each of the realms of existence, we should develop a deep sense of aversion for all experience within samsara and develop deep renunciation. Then we will begin to really examine exactly what the causes are that lead to such miseries and frustrations. Therefore the question of the second truth, the truth of the origin of suffering, comes next.

The Truth of Origin

Delusion is the chief cause of rebirth in samsara. Without delusions karmic actions would not have the power to produce rebirth; they would be like seeds that have been burned. It is very important to seek the antidotes to the delusions, and that in turn depends upon whether or not you have identified the delusions properly. Therefore, we should be very clear about the general and individual characteristics of the delusions. As the

First Dalai Lama said, tame the one enemy within, which is delusion. External enemies might seem very harmful, but in future lives they could turn into our friends. Even now they provide us with the opportunity to practice patience and compassion because we are all basically the same: we all want happiness and do not want suffering. But the inner enemy, the enemy of delusion, has no positive qualities; it is only to be fought and destroyed. We thus have to identify the enemy properly and see how it operates. Any mental state that destroys calmness of mind and brings about mental misery, which upsets, afflicts, and torments the mind, is said to be a delusion.

Let us identify some of the chief delusions. First, there is attachment, which is the strong desire for beautiful persons, beautiful things, or pleasurable experiences. Attachment is very difficult to get rid of; it is as if your mind has become fixed to the object. Another delusion is anger. When people become angry, we can immediately see that they lose their composure; their faces become red and wrinkled, and even their eyes become red. The object of anger, whether animate or inanimate, is something found to be undesirable and repulsive. Anger is a very untamed state of mind, very rough and uneven. Another delusion, pride, is a state of mind in which one feels conceited about one's own status, position, and knowledge, based on a self-centered attitude. Regardless of whether one has really achieved something or not, one feels inflated. Someone who has very deep pride is very pompous and appears very inflated. Next is ignorance, which misconceives the identity of the Four Noble Truths, the law of karma, and so forth. In this particular context, ignorance refers to a mental factor that is totally ignorant of the nature of the Three Jewels and the law of karma. The delusion of doubt is wavering thought concerning whether there are Four Noble Truths or not, whether there is a law of karma or not.

Another category of delusions is wrong views, active misconceptions about the nature of reality. The first of these is a state of mind that focuses on one's self and misconceives it to be truly or substantially existent— to imagine that within our impermanent bodies and minds there is some kind of permanent, autonomous self. Other types of wrong view would hold that there is no life after death, no law of karma, and no Three Jewels. Based on the mistaken view of self, the other delusions arise. For example, if there is a coiled rope and it is a little dark, you might misidentify that coiled rope as a snake. Then the mistaken idea that the rope was a snake would set off all kinds of reactions in your mind, such as fear, and would lead to all sorts of actions, such as running out of the house or trying to kill the snake, all based on a simple misapprehension. In the same manner, we mistakenly believe that the body and mind possess some kind of self, and as a result all the other delusions, like desire and anger, follow. Due to this self-centered attitude, this misconception of self, we discriminate between ourselves and others. Then, based on how others treat us, we hold some to be dear and feel attachment for them and hold others to be distant and classify them as enemies. We then have experiences of anger and hatred, and, focused upon ourselves, we become inflated and proud. Then, if the grip of the misconception of self is very strong, we may begin to question the validity of the Buddha himself who taught selflessness. We therefore may begin to doubt the law of karma, the Four Noble Truths, the Three Jewels. These wrong views lead to doubts. All of this arises because of the mistaken belief in an intrinsically existent self.

When delusion arises within you it upsets your calmness, your presence of mind, and it also clouds your judgment of people. It leaves a very strong imprint. It harms not only you but others as well. For example, if you are so angry that you begin to hit people, you cause trouble for your neighbors. Anger will decrease your power of virtue and will cause you to lose your possessions and your friends. When someone is under the sway of anger, he or she really loses the characteristics of a human being. We humans are naturally equipped with a very sophisticated brain, and we have the power to judge what is right and wrong and weigh the pros and cons of a situation. We have that natural gift, which is unique to human beings compared to other forms of existence, but when we are under the strong influence of delusion, we lose that power. Although we might decide to do something, we lose the power of judgment. Taming the mind is the most important task of one's life.

The Truth of Cessation

As Tsong-kha-pa said, all the realms in which we might take rebirth in the cycle of existence, from the peak of existence to the lowest hell, have the nature of suffering. These sufferings do not come about without any cause, nor are they created by some kind of almighty god. They are products of our own delusions and karmic actions prompted by untamed states of mind. The root cause of all suffering is the ignorance that misconceives the nature of phenomena and apprehends oneself as self-existent. This ignorance leads us to exaggerate the status of phenomena and create the categories of self and others. These bring about experiences of desire and hatred, which in turn result in all sorts of negative actions. These in turn bring about all our undesirable sufferings. If we do not want these sufferings we should determine whether or not it is possible to get rid of them. If the ignorance that misconceives the self is a mistaken consciousness, it can be eliminated by correcting the mistake. This can be accomplished by generating within our minds a wisdom that realizes the direct opposite of that state of mind, a wisdom realizing that there is no such intrinsically existent self. When we compare these two states of mind—one believing in an intrinsically existent self, the other perceiving the absence of such a self—the apprehension of self might initially appear very strong and powerful. But because it is a mistaken consciousness, it lacks logical support. The other type of mind, the understanding of selflessness, might be very weak at the initial stage, but it has logical support. Sooner or later this wisdom realizing selflessness is going to gain the upper hand. The truth at the initial stage may not be very obvious, but as we get closer to it, it becomes increasingly self-evident. Something false at the initial stage might seem very vivid and firm, but eventually, as we probe it further, it becomes more flimsy and eventually dissolves.

Delusion is separate from consciousness; it is not part of the essential nature of mind. For example, someone who might be very short-tempered does have some moments of peace of mind. Just being a very angry person does not mean that one has to be angry all the time. Therefore, when these deluded states of mind like hatred and desire arise within us, they are really very forceful and strong, but it is never the case that they will remain manifest for as long as we are conscious. Another fact is that we cannot possibly have two opposing types of mental state focused upon one object at the same time, like a very deep hatred toward someone and at the same time a very deep feeling of pity toward that person.

Within our minds there are many different aspects, very subtle ones, some negative, some positive. Within these two polarities we find that it is also obvious that the more we enhance and increase our familiarity with one side, the weaker the grip of the other side becomes. Therefore, the stains and delusions within our minds can be eliminated. Our own experiences testify that some people when young are really very short-tempered and easily provoked, but later they turn into very gentle people. This shows that it is possible to change our mental states. As we familiarize our minds with love and compassion, the strength of anger will gradually decrease.

The Truth of the Path

Having seen that all experience in the cycle of existence has a nature of suffering, we should develop a genuine wish to gain liberation from it. Motivated by that wish, we should enter the path of the three trainings: the trainings of morality, concentration, and wisdom. Among these three, the antidote that will eliminate the delusions is the wisdom realizing selflessness. For that purpose, we first require the mental stability of concentration as the basis, and that in turn depends upon the observance of pure morality. Therefore, we need training in morality as well. At the initial stage, the first priority should be given to the practice of morality; that is the immediate need.

Tsong-kha-pa says that mindfulness and introspection are the foundation of the entire Dharma. In order to have a pure observance of morality, the faculties of introspection and proper mindfulness are required.

For laymen and laywomen the observance of pure morality, refraining from the ten negative actions, is the foundation of the practice of the path leading to enlightenment. If we do not consider practical needs, like the observance of morality, but instead go in search of more sophisticated practices, our practice will be simply a sham and not really very serious. With the practice of these three trainings, we should work for the achievement of liberation, not just for ourselves alone but also for other sentient beings.

Human existence is said to be the best form of existence to practice the Dharma and try to bring an end to this cycle. Among human beings, the life of laypeople is beset with all sorts of troubles and problems, and they are more involved with worldly activities that are not very conducive to the practice of the Dharma. Life as a monk or nun is said to be far more conducive to the practice of the Dharma, to put an end to this cycle of existence. Tsong-kha-pa says that to reflect upon the faults and the disadvantages of lay life and the advantages of monks' and nuns' life reinforces your commitment to such a life if you already are a monk or nun. If someone has not yet chosen such a way of life, such reflection leaves a very strong karmic imprint on one's mind so that later one will have the chance to lead such a life. In lay life, if you are too wealthy, your life will be beset with problems and worries about protecting your wealth; if you are poor, then your life will just be involved in searching for material sustenance. To have many material possessions and not be content is not the way of life for a monk or nun. Monks and nuns should not be involved in business unless they have fallen into some kind of debt. Doing business and having too much involvement in trying to raise money when you have sufficient provisions should really be avoided. If you do not live according to the monastic way of life, with modesty and contentment, there is hardly any difference between laypeople and monks and nuns apart from the mere external appearance of different types of clothes.

There was a monk from Ganden monastery who was a very serious meditator. He had taken a pledge never to live under a roof and had done that for many years. He told me that one day he was meditating when a big snake crawled in front of him and just gazed at him. The meditator looked back at the snake and started to say some religious words. I found it quite funny, because it seemed as if the meditator was giving teachings to the snake. He told me that the snake looked at him for a long time and then went gently away.

The importance of moral discipline was emphasized by the Buddha himself. When he was passing away, the Buddha was asked who would succeed him, and he said that the practice of morality should be the guide and the master of the entire Buddhist doctrine. He named moral discipline as his successor.

In order to overcome the abundance of delusions, it is important to check your own mind, and whatever emotion is more forceful and abundant should be given first priority. For example, some people are very attached to sensual pleasures, some people are very short-tempered, some people are very ignorant and lazy. You should check your own personality and try to overcome whatever emotion is most obvious and strong within your mind. As explained earlier, you should really make an effort to ensure that none of your vows are broken. However, if you find that some vows have been transgressed, you should not leave them like that but rather should apply the necessary procedures and immediately restore and purify them. Purification of the transgression should always be accompanied by a very deep resolve not to repeat it; having the notion that "it does not matter what I do because even if I transgress the vows I can restore them" is really very dangerous, like deliberately eating poison thinking that you can be cured.

Having realized the importance of morality and reflected on how peaceful it would be if you could be free of these delusions, then, as explained earlier, you should first identify the delusions individually. Having identified them, reflect upon their destructive nature, and then apply mindfulness and the power of introspection. Whichever delusions are more forceful and obvious should be countered immediately, just like hitting whatever sticks out with a hammer. If you simply leave them they will do real harm to yourself and others. Delusion might seem very forceful, but it is not that powerful if you analyze it carefully. I once asked one of my lamas if the delusions were truly weak, because sometimes they seem so strong. He answered that delusions are weak because you do not need

nuclear weapons to destroy them. I began to understand what he meant. All we are lacking in order to
combat the delusions successfully is the necessary will
and effort. Defeating our enemies, the delusions, is
largely a matter of having the right attitude. Our state
of mind is so important that whenever the Indian master Atisha met someone, the first question he would
ask was, "Do you have a kind heart today?" You might
defeat ordinary enemies once, but they can regroup
and attack again. But once the delusions are eliminated, there is no possibility of resurgence.

Whatever realization you gain from your practice of
the Dharma should be valued and judged on the basis
of whether your commitment to the law of karma has
increased and, as a result, whether your practice of
morality has become pure and whether the force of
delusions, like ignorance, hatred, and desire, has de-
creased within you. If you notice that as a result of
your practice you have managed to change your mind
and have overcome some of the gross manifestations of
the delusions, like anger, hatred, ignorance, and desire,
that really is a great achievement. As Shantideva says,
ordinary heroes who kill their enemies are not really
heroes because the people they kill would have died
sooner or later; they are actually killing corpses. But
someone who is fighting the delusions and is able to
kill that enemy is a hero in the true sense of the word.

CHAPTER · 9

THE BODHISATTVA

IDEAL

Being content with the achievement of
liberation from the cycle of existence is not
enough. Even speaking from the viewpoint

of your own aims, it is the omniscient state of Buddhahood that is the complete fulfillment of your own welfare. After having developed the wish to achieve liberation and having undertaken practice of the three
trainings, instead of being concerned with the achievement of your own personal liberation, it is better for
intelligent practitioners to meditate on the altruistic
aspiration to Buddhahood, called bodhichitta, right
from the outset and enter the Mahayana, the Great
Vehicle. If you see people who are under the constant
sway of delusions and undergoing suffering, yet you
do not work for their benefit, it is really very unfair and
disappointing. You should not be content with working for your own personal benefit alone. You should
think in broader terms and try to work for the benefit

of many people. This is what distinguishes human beings from animals, because the wish to work for the benefit of oneself and one's relations is something that even animals do. The unique feature of human beings is that they work for the benefit of others, not being concerned with their own welfare alone. That is the beauty and the specialty of a human being.

People like the American president Lincoln and the Indian leader Mahatma Gandhi are regarded as really great men because they did not think of themselves alone but worked for the benefit of the people. They thought of the entire human society, and they struggled and fought for the rights of the poor. Take the example of Mahatma Gandhi: after gaining Indian independence he just remained as an ordinary citizen, never taking any position, such as prime minister. That is the mark of a distinguished person. Mao at first worked very hard for the rights of the masses, but after gaining power, he himself became a member of the very same class he had fought against. He succumbed to power and became utterly totalitarian, taking even the slightest dissent as a great personal offense. Once Mao was praised, but now that people have become disillusioned, more and more things are revealed.

When the sun shines, it shines without any discrimination; it shines on every point of the country, every nook and corner. We should be like that. We practitioners of the Mahayana should not be concerned with our own benefit but with a single-pointed mind should develop the courageous altruistic attitude, taking upon our own shoulders the responsibility of working for all sentient beings.

Bodhichitta, the compassionate wish to achieve Buddhahood for the sake of others, is the entrance to the Mahayana path. When you cultivate bodhichitta, even though you might not make any further progress on the path, you become a Mahayanist, but the moment bodhichitta degenerates, even though you might have very high realizations, you fall from the ranks of the Mahayana. Shantideva says that the moment you develop bodhichitta, even though you might be living in a lower realm of existence, you will be called a bodhisattva, a child of the Buddhas. As a result of bodhichitta, you will be able to purify negativities very easily and be able to fulfill your aims. You will be invulnerable to interferences and harm, because if you have this faculty of bodhichitta, you regard other people as more important and precious than your own life. When harmful spirits realize this, they hesitate to harm you. As a result of bodhichitta, if you are able to purify negativities and accumulate great stores of merit, you will encounter favorable circumstances that are necessary for making speedy progress on the path. Bodhichitta and compassion are the very sources and foundations of all the goodness in this world and nirvana. You should regard bodhichitta as the essence of your practice and should not leave it only at an intellectual level; you should not be satisfied with your practice of bodhichitta if it consists merely of the recitation of a few verses at the beginning of a meditation session. You should try to generate it through experience.

Tsong-kha-pa says that if you have an authentic aspiration to enlightenment, then any act of goodness, even something minor like giving grain to a crow, becomes a bodhisattva deed. However, if you lack this motivating factor, even though you might make offerings of an entire universe filled with jewels to other sentient beings, it will not be the deed of a bodhisattva. If your practice of bodhichitta is not successful, no matter how long you try to practice the Dharma, it will be a very slow and laborious process, like cutting grass with a blunt tool. But if you have a perfect and successful realization of bodhichitta, even though it may take some time to make that your primary motive, all of your practices will be very powerful. If you do not repeatedly reinforce your compassion, improving and enhancing it, there is a great danger of losing your courage and becoming depressed, because sentient beings are infinite. There are many hostile sentient beings who, instead of repaying your kindness, will try to harm you. Therefore, you should not be satisfied with a single experience of compassion but should really work to enhance it to the point where your compassion is deeply rooted. If that happens, you will not care much about hardships, and as a result you will never be depressed by circumstances when you work for the benefit of others. It is because of the force of compassion that the Buddhas remain committed to working for the benefit of other sentient beings. The Buddha said that bodhisattvas do not need to be concerned with many aspects of the path; they need not practice many other things. It is by one practice alone that Buddhahood will be in the palm of your hand. That one practice is great compassion, meaning the desire to become enlightened in order to liberate all other sentient beings. In order to generate this aspiration to enlightenment it is not enough to have great compassion and love, wishing sentient beings to be free of suffering. In addition, what is required is the sense of personal responsibility to shoulder the task of freeing them from sufferings and providing them with happiness.

When we reflect upon the suffering nature of sentient beings, we might be able to develop the wish that they be free from such sufferings. In order to discover a warm and kind heart that is forceful, stable, and firm, it is very important first of all to have an affectionate attitude toward sentient beings, regarding them as precious and dear. The more affection you feel toward other sentient beings and the more you hold them dear, the better you will be able to develop genuine compassion for them. Normally, when we let our natural reactions follow their own course, we find it unbearable to see the sufferings of our relatives and friends. We tend to delight in the misfortunes and failures of our enemies, and we tend to remain indifferent to people we do not know. Our emotions fluctuate in relation to these different people. The more we regard a person as close and dear to us, the stronger our feeling of being unable to bear it when that person suffers.

In order to equalize your feelings, visualize three people in front of you: a very close friend, an enemy, and a neutral person. Having visualized these three people, let your mind react naturally. You will find that your mind reacts in an unbalanced way. You find yourself attached to the friend and repelled by the enemy, and your attitude to the third person is totally indifferent. Then, examine why you react in such a manner. Friends might be friends now, but they may have been our enemies in the past, and they could be our enemies in the future. Those whom we call enemies now may have been our best friends or relatives in the past and could also turn out to be the same in the future. What is the point of making such discriminations? Friends are those whom we wish to have happiness and to enjoy life. We wish them happiness and success because they are our relatives and friends and have been good to us. But in the future they could turn out to be our enemies, and even in this life they could turn against us. Similarly, when we react to our enemies, we tend to react in a very negative manner, wishing instinctively, deep down, that they face misfortune, hardship, and failure. We react like that because we think that they have harmed us. But even though they might actually be harmful at present, they could turn out to be our friends in the future. There is no certainty, no totally reliable or permanent friend or enemy. Like-

wise, although the neutral person is totally uncon-
cerned with us and we are indifferent to him or her in
turn, in the past that person may have been either our
friend or enemy. If you train your mind this way, you
will come to see all people in the same light, and gradually such a drastic discrimination among the three
types of people will begin to fade. You should extend
this practice to include everyone, eventually encom-
passing all sentient beings. That is how you develop
equanimity. This is not to suggest that we do not have
friends and enemies. What we are concerned with here
is to offset our drastic, imbalanced emotional reactions
to others. This equanimity is very important; it is like
first leveling the ground before cultivating it. Although
equanimity itself is not a great realization, if you have
that foundation, further practices become very successful.

After developing equanimity, the first of the cause-
and-effect precepts for creating the aspiration to enlightenment is the recognition that all sentient beings
have been our mother in a past life. This is because
there is no beginning to the cycle of existence. Because
life in the cycle of rebirth is beginningless, our own
lives are also beginningless. Life and death succeed
each other without any interruption. Whenever we
take on a body, we require a mother. Since the cycle of
existence has no beginning, there is no sentient being
we can point to and say, "That person has not been
my mother in the past." Not only have they been our
mothers in the past, but also they will be our mothers

in the future. If you are able to develop deep conviction in this fact, it will be quite easy to recollect and reflect upon their great kindness and then develop the wish to repay their kindness. Although it is usually recommended that you see all sentient beings as your mother, you should do this meditation according to your own experience. For example, some people feel closer to their father. The person to whom you feel closest and regard as most kind should be taken as the model. There is not a single sentient being who has not been either our mother or father or relative in the past. The fact that we do not remember or recognize them does not mean that they have not been our mothers. For example, even in this lifetime there are cases of parents and children being separated when the children are very young. Later, these children are unable to recognize their parents.

The next precept is to reflect on the kindness of all sentient beings. This meditation is said to be most successful if, after having recognized all the other sentient beings as your mother, you recollect their kindness, taking your own mother as an example. Visualize your mother in front of you, and reflect that she has been your mother not only in this lifetime but also numerous times in the past. Then think of how kind she has been to you, how she has protected you from danger and how she has helped you, how in this life she first conceived you and even during the pregnancy she took great care of you. She looked after you with no sense of hesitation. She was willing to give up her possessions for your sake, and she was willing to use devious and irreligious means to obtain what you needed with no care for the hardships it caused her. Her commitment and love for her child was such that she would prefer to fall ill herself rather than have her child become sick. You should single-pointedly meditate on her great kindness. When you develop a deep feeling of indebtedness to your mother for her great kindness by reflecting this way, you should apply the same method to other people who have been kind to you, such as your friends and relatives. Eventually you can extend it to include neutral persons. If you are able to develop that same kind of feeling for neutral persons, shift it to your own enemy as well. Gradually include all other sentient beings within the sphere of your recognition of kindness.

Next is meditation on repaying their kindness. You should understand that it is only because of our constantly changing lives that we are not able to recognize that all sentient beings have been our kind mothers, parents, and relatives. Now they are protectorless; they have no refuge. If we see their suffering and their helplessness and then still work for our own benefit and personal liberation alone, we will not only be acting unfairly, but also extremely ungratefully. You should develop a deep sense of commitment that you will never abandon them but will instead repay their kindness. Even in a worldly sense, if someone does not repay the kindness of people but acts against them, he or she is regarded as a very bad and ungrateful person. How then can a Mahayana practitioner completely neglect the welfare of other sentient beings and not think of repaying their kindness?

Imagine your mother, mentally unstable, blind, and without any guide, walking toward a cliff. She calls out to her own child nearby, her only refuge, in whom she places her hopes. If her own child does not help her, who is going to? We should reflect on the idea that since the beginning of time sentient beings have been mentally unstable because they have been slaves of delusion, they lack the eye of wisdom to see the path leading to nirvana and enlightenment, and they lack the necessary guidance of a spiritual teacher. Moment by moment they are indulging in negative actions, which will eventually bring about their downfall. If these mothers cannot seek help from their children, in whom can they place their hope? Feeling a sense of responsibility, you should repay the great kindness of the mother.

Next is the meditation on love. The Buddhist definition of love is the wish that all sentient beings may enjoy happiness and never be parted from happiness. It is said that meditation on love even for a moment far exceeds the merits accumulated through making infinite offerings to infinite Buddhas. It was by the power of meditation on love that the Buddha defeated the hosts of demons who tried to keep him from his goal. Meditation on love is the supreme protection. The actual sequence of meditation on love is that first you should cultivate love directed toward your own friends and relatives, then you should shift that attention to neutral persons, then on to your enemies as well. Then gradually include all other sentient beings whom you encounter.

Next is meditation on compassion. There are two types of compassion; one is just a wish that sentient beings be free of suffering, and the other is more powerful: "I shall take the responsibility for freeing sentient beings from suffering." First you should meditate on your own parents, friends, and relatives and then shift that attention to neutral persons and eventually to your enemies, so that eventually all sentient beings you encounter will be a part of your meditation. This has great significance because when you are able to extend your meditation to all sentient beings, your compassion and love will become so pervasive that the moment you see suffering, compassion will spontaneously arise. Otherwise, if you try to meditate on compassion and love for all sentient beings, thinking about "all sentient beings" without first identifying them individually, your idea of "all sentient beings" will be very vague, and your compassion will not be very strong and firm. When you meet with certain individuals, you will begin to doubt whether you really wish them to enjoy happiness. On the other hand, if you cultivate compassion in a gradual process, first of all picking out individual categories of people and making a very special effort to cultivate that kind of love and compassion focused on your enemy, who is the most difficult object, then having love and compassion toward others will become very easy, and your compassion will be able to withstand any circumstances you might meet.

In the actual meditation you should contemplate how sentient beings, like yourself, rotate in the cycle of existence tormented by all types of sufferings. To be successful in developing love and compassion, it is very important to understand and realize the faults and defects of the cycle of existence. If you are able to do that in terms of your own observations, you can extend your understanding to other sentient beings through experience. Otherwise, if you have not developed renunciation yourself and a sense of aversion for the entire range of experience within this cycle of existence, there is no way you can cultivate compassion. Renunciation is indispensable for the cultivation of compassion. Compassion and renunciation differ only in their object: renunciation is focused upon yourself; it is the wish that you be liberated from suffering. Compassion is directed toward other sentient beings; it is the wish that all beings be liberated from suffering.

It is very important to study and understand the many types of sufferings. Having gained extensive knowledge by reading many texts and thinking a lot, you should contemplate the faults and defects of the cycle of life and death and how sentient beings in this cycle of existence spin through this chain reaction. For example, in scientific laboratories, guinea pigs are tortured with all sorts of equipment. To understand how the brain operates, scientists have to experiment on animals. It is a very strange situation, because their primary aim is to help and prolong the life of human beings. In a way it is a noble aim, but it is also difficult to justify. Although they may use tranquilizers, scientists do these kinds of experiments without any sense of compassion or mercy for the animals. In the West there are groups who protest against such treatment of animals, not out of religious sentiments but out of their compassionate attitude toward animals. I support this effort.

Initially it might prove quite difficult to generate any experience of compassion for all beings, but once you begin to develop it, it will become firm, genuine, and unshakable, because it is based on a firm foundation of knowledge and reason. If you have some experience of compassion, it is really important to try to stabilize it by reinforcing it with reasons and extensive understanding. Merely depending upon some kind of intuition alone is not very reliable, because there is a danger that afterward that kind of experience will disappear without a trace. This is true not only of meditation on compassion and love, but for all the other practices as well.

As a result of your continuous meditation and contemplation, your feeling of compassion toward other sentient beings will become as intense as the love of a mother toward her only child when she sees him or her suffering from an illness. The child's suffering would cause her worry and pain, and day and night she would have the natural wish that her son or daughter be well.

If your attitude toward any other sentient being is such that, regardless of whether or not they are related to you, the moment you see any suffering you are able to develop an equally intense compassion toward all other sentient beings without partiality, that is the sign of having achieved and developed compassion. This applies to love as well. Such love and compassion will lead naturally, without any effort, to the superior attitude of taking upon your own shoulders the responsibility of working for the benefit of other sentient beings, which in turn leads to the eventual realization of the aspiration to enlightenment.

In meditating on repaying kindness you have reflected on the great kindness of the mother sentient beings and on the necessity of working for their benefit. Here the primary concern is to cultivate a deep-felt sense of responsibility to work for their benefit and shoulder the task of relieving sentient beings of suffering and providing them with happiness. Throughout your daily life and activities, wherever the occasion arises, you should immediately seize that opportunity to train in this meditation. Only then can you begin to hope for progress in the realization. The Indian poet Chandragomin (sixth century C.E.) said that it is stupid to expect to change the taste of a very sour fruit simply by adding one or two drops of sugar cane. In the same way, we cannot expect the taste of the mind, which is so contaminated with the sour flavor of delusion, to be instantly changed into the sweet taste of bodhichitta and compassion, just by one or two meditations. Sustained effort and continuity are really very important.

In the last step, the actual development of bodhi-chitta, the mind aspiring to achieve enlightenment for others, you should not be satisfied by seeing the importance of enlightenment for the sake of others alone. There is no way to fulfill that ultimate aim without your achievement of the omniscient state of Buddha-hood, from which you can best benefit others. You should develop a very deep, heartfelt faith in the enlightened state, and that will lead to a genuine aspiration to achieve it. Generally speaking, there are many causes and conditions for the cultivation of bodhi-chitta, but chief among all of them is compassion.

We should realize that the purpose of taking birth in this world is to help others. If we cannot do that, at least we should not harm other living beings. Even people who are opposed to religion speak highly of the altruistic attitude. Although the Chinese Communists are ideologically opposed to religion, they talk of the wish to work for the welfare of the masses. If these people truly had an altruistic attitude, they would be able to fulfill the wish for a perfect socialist state. On the other hand, if they continue to use violent methods to enforce a totalitarian system, there is no way that they can bring about what they are looking for. Nations have diverse political systems, but an essential factor in most societies is the altruistic attitude—the wish to work for others, for the welfare of the majority. The altruistic attitude is the root of happiness within the human community. All the major religions of the world encourage cultivation of an altruistic attitude, irrespective of their different philosophical systems. In short, if you cultivate the altruistic attitude, it not only helps you by providing peace of mind, it also creates a peaceful atmosphere around you. That is one of the practical results that you can see. The ultimate purpose of cultivating the altruistic attitude is to achieve the enlightened state so that you will be able to work for the total fulfillment of the wishes of other beings. Therefore, the Buddha has not left the importance of cultivating bodhichitta as a matter of simple advice; he has also shown the techniques and means by which we can develop such an altruistic aspiration.

Once we have taken rebirth in this world, as long as we are human beings we depend for our survival on other human beings. We cannot survive independently. That is the nature of being human. Therefore, we should help our fellow human beings and relieve them of their sufferings, both physical and mental. That is the proper way to treat our fellow human beings. Insects like bees and ants do not have a system of education, but in practical terms, because they have to depend upon each other for their survival, they somehow help each other, regardless of whether they have a strong sense of affection and compassion. When ants get a large piece of bread, they help each other to carry it. Human beings depend for their survival on their fellow human beings yet do not treat each other as fellow human beings. All human beings have a natural tendency to wish for the experience of happiness and to avoid suffering. Taking that into account, it is very important to cultivate an altruistic attitude to help others.

We have obtained this life as a human being. Whether we make it worthwhile or not depends upon our own mental attitude. If we adopt a devious attitude but show a benevolent and kind face, we are making a mistake. If we have this altruistic attitude and treat others as they deserve to be treated, then our own happiness is assured as a by-product of working for the happiness of others. When we experience happiness, we should rejoice in the fact that it is the consequence of virtuous actions we have committed in the past. At the same time, we should dedicate that virtue to the happiness of all sentient beings in the hope that they may experience this type of happiness as well. If we undergo suffering, we should realize that it is the consequence of nonvirtuous actions that we have committed in the past, and we should develop a wish that through our experience of this suffering, all the sufferings that other sentient beings have to undergo in the future may be avoided. Pledge that whether you achieve enlightenment or not, you will work for the welfare of other sentient beings come what may. Having received instructions on the method of overcoming the self-centered attitude, you can die without regret. When I give explanations of my practice in aspiring to develop this aspiration to enlightenment, I feel very fortunate to be doing so. My mouth and tongue have served their purpose. Listeners and readers should rejoice at the great fortune of becoming acquainted with such marvelous teachings whose practice bestows benefits both now and in the future.

The practice of bodhichitta is indispensable for someone who wishes to achieve enlightenment. All the Buddhas and bodhisattvas of the past have achieved these high realizations by cultivating this altruistic attitude. Some ideologies lose their relevance as time passes. The Buddha taught that life is our most cherished possession and that we should treat the lives of others as more important and precious than our own. This kind of message and teaching retains its relevance throughout the ages. In this modern age when there is a great danger of the destruction of the entire world, we find the message of the Buddha more and more relevant.

The other method for developing the altruistic aspiration to enlightenment is the equalizing and exchanging of self and others. The first step in this practice is to recognize the advantages of exchanging oneself for others and the disadvantages of not doing so. All the good qualities in this universe are the product of cherishing the welfare of others, and all the frustrations and confusions and sufferings are products and consequences of selfish attitudes. But is it possible to exchange oneself for others? Our experience testifies that we can change our attitude toward certain types of people whom we formerly found repulsive and fearful, that when we get closer to such persons and understand them, we can change our attitude. Exchanging self and others does not mean that you physically change yourself into others but rather that the attitude that you have about yourself is applied to others. The strong cherishing that you feel for yourself should now be shifted to others, so that you will have a natural tendency to work for the welfare of others instead of yourself.

There are two main obstacles to developing such an attitude. The first is this strong discrimination between self and others, regarding self and others as totally independent and separate. In fact, self and other are relative, like "this side of the mountain" and "that side of the mountain." From my perspective, I am self and you are other, but from your perspective, you are self and I am other. We also have a natural feeling of indifference because we feel that the happiness and suffering of others is not our business; they do not matter to us. Then we have to remember that there are certain types of people, like our relatives, whom we hold very dear. Even though your relatives are not you, the sufferings and happiness they experience do affect you. Also, despite the fact that our bodies consist of many parts—head, hands, legs—we treat our own bodies, collections of parts, as very precious. In the same way, we should look at what unites us, the common feature that all the sentient beings like ourselves share, the natural wish to achieve happiness and avoid sufferings. We regard a person who gives up his or her life for the sake of others as noble, but we think that it is foolish to sacrifice ten people to save one. This has nothing to do with religion; it is simply a human response. Therefore, to give up the rights, benefits, and privileges of the few for the sake of the many is right and fair. This is what the Buddha teaches—that to give up the privileges and rights of one individual for the welfare of all other beings, who are as infinite as space, is right and fair.

When we try to practice the exchange of self and other, we meet strong resistance from our own natural tendency and self-centered attitude. It is very important that we overcome them. The idea that the happiness and sufferings of others do not matter to me, so there is no need for me to work for others, is a significant obstacle. But we should reflect that although we are not the same persons now that we will be twenty years from now, it would be foolish for us not to be concerned for the ones we will be in the future. It would be foolish to do things that will later cause him or her to suffer. We should also reflect that when you step on a thorn and hurt your foot, one of your hands removes the thorn, even though that hand is not undergoing suffering. It is only because of familiarity and habituation that we have this strong clinging to our own selves and regard anything that is related to ourselves as very precious and something to be cherished. Through constant familiarity we can develop just as strong an attitude cherishing the welfare of others. Although we have been working to achieve happiness and be free of suffering since beginningless time, our self-centered attitude has caused us to undergo incredible pain. If, at some time in the past, we had been able to change this attitude and instead of cherishing ourselves we had cherished the welfare of others and worked for their happiness, then we would have achieved the bliss of Buddhahood by now.

Therefore, we should decide, "From now on I shall dedicate myself, even my body, for the welfare of others. From now on, I will not work for my own happiness but rather for the happiness of others. From now on others are like my master; my body will obey and take orders from others instead of myself." Reflecting upon the great disadvantages and harms of the selfish attitude, you should develop a strong determination, saying to the self-cherishing attitude, "Your domination of my mind is a thing of the past. From now on I will not obey your orders. You have only done me great harm by your devious means. From now on do not pretend that you are working for my own happiness, because I have realized that you are the great enemy and the source of all my frustrations and sufferings. If I do not abandon you and work for others, you will again plunge me into the sufferings of unfortunate rebirth." Understand that a self-centered attitude is the source of all suffering, and concern for others is the source of all happiness and goodness.

If you meet ten equally poor beggars, it is wrong to make distinctions among them, deciding that some are more deserving than others. If there are ten equally sick persons, it is senseless to start making discriminations among them. Similarly, you should develop an equal attitude toward all the other sentient beings, who either are suffering or who have the potential to suffer. These sentient beings have shown you boundless kindness in the past. From a religious point of view, even the enemy is kind because he or she provides you with the opportunity to develop patience. All of us have the same nature, and all of us are suffering the same fate; there is no point in being antagonistic and unfriendly to each other. The Buddhas see only the delusions as faults to be eliminated; they never discriminate among the sentient beings who are beset by delusions, helping some and not helping others. If some beings were intrinsically evil, the Buddhas would see this and would abandon such people. Because they, who see reality exactly as it is, do not act this way, we can conclude that evil is a temporary affliction that can be eliminated. It is said that if the Buddha was flanked by two people, one striking the Buddha with a weapon and the other massaging the Buddha with oil, he would not favor one over the other.

Thus in the ultimate sense enemies and friends do not exist. This does not mean that there are not people who sometimes help us and others who sometimes harm us. What we are concerned with here is trying to overcome our fluctuating emotions. We should reflect upon the relativity of friends and enemies in order to reduce the grip of emotional reactions. We can then more easily identify the great advantages of cherishing others—the door to the achievement of all good qualities. We will then naturally wish to work for others, and the indifference that we previously felt for others can now be applied to our own welfare. The strong emotional attachment normally associated with our own welfare in the past can now be transferred to others.

If we think carefully, we can see that even the achievement of our own enlightenment very much depends on others. Without the practice of the three trainings in ethics, meditation, and wisdom, there is no way we can achieve nirvana. The practice of the three trainings begins with morality, such as vowing not to kill. If there were no other sentient beings, how could we refrain from killing them? All these practices depend upon the contribution of others. In short, right from the beginning of our conception in the womb up to now, we have been entirely dependent upon the kindness and contribution of others. A Tibetan would not enjoy drinking Tibetan tea without the contribution of animals like the female yak. Milk is the natural right of the calf, but we take it away and make it into butter. Without other beings' contributions, we would not have these things. The same is true of shelter and food and especially fame. In this modern world, without the activities of journalists, no one could become famous. Even if one person shouts out loud, he or she will not become famous that way.

We find that our very survival is something that is dependent upon others. This is true in the world, and it is true on the path: everything depends upon the contribution and kindness of others. So if we reflect along such lines, our recollection of the kindness of others will have a greater dimension. I often remark that if you would like to be selfish, you should do it in a very intelligent way. The stupid way to be selfish is the way we always have worked, seeking happiness for ourselves alone and in the process becoming more and more miserable. The intelligent way to be selfish is to work for the welfare of others, because you become a Buddha in the process.

In order never to separate from the aspiration to become a Buddha for the sake of others, even in future lifetimes, we have to maintain certain kinds of training. Specifically, we should abandon the four negative actions and undertake the practice of the four virtuous actions associated with this training. The first negative action is deceiving your spiritual master, especially by telling lies. The second negative action is causing a religious practitioner who has no regret about his or her past virtuous actions to develop such regret because of something that you say. The third negative action is to insult bodhisattvas, beings who have generated bodhichitta, by belittling them and insulting them. This is a negative action we are very prone to commit, because it is very difficult to say who is a bodhisattva and who is not. We should be very careful to avoid this. The Perfection of Wisdom Sutras explain the gravity of generating anger. If you realize that you have lost your temper toward a bodhisattva, it is very important to regret it immediately and engage in means of purifying your negative action, with a strong resolve never to indulge in such actions in the future. The greatest stumbling block in your cultivation of compassion and the aspiration to enlightenment is hatred toward others. The fourth negative action is deceiving others without any sense of conscience, especially concealing your own faults and pretending to have high realizations.

The four virtuous actions are the opposite of these four. The first is never to lie to any living being. There are a few exceptions where you might have to tell lies in order to protect the Dharma or other people, but otherwise you should avoid telling lies to anybody. The second virtuous action is to be honest, and the third is to praise and have high regard for bodhisattvas, who are constantly working for others. Again, it is very difficult to assess who is and who is not a bodhisattva, so it is safer to develop a strong sense of respect toward all sentient beings and always speak highly of them and praise their positive qualities. The fourth virtuous action is exhorting others to work for the achievement of Buddhahood, the completely enlightened state.

CHAPTER 10

THE BODHISATTVA
DEEDS

*Although the generation of the aspirational
aspect of the bodhichitta alone is very
remarkable and a virtuous action in itself,*

that alone will not fulfill your aim of achieving Buddhahood. It is important to engage in the practice of
the bodhisattva deeds. These deeds, called the six perfections, constitute the essential and comprehensive
path to enlightenment, combining method and wisdom. The Buddha himself said that by the force of
their wisdom bodhisattvas abandon all the delusions,
but by the force of their compassionate method they
never abandon sentient beings. These two aspects of
the path should always be undertaken in combination,
never in isolation. The entire practice of the bodhisattva is classified under the six perfections, which
are generosity, ethics, patience, effort, concentration,
and wisdom.

To fulfill the wishes of others it is very important to engage in the practice of generosity, and generosity itself should be reinforced by the pure observance of ethics, abstaining from inflicting harm upon others. Ethical practice itself should be completed by the practice of patience, because you should have forbearance toward harm inflicted upon you by others. In order to engage in such practices, you must have strong effort. Without concentration, your practice will not be powerful. And without wisdom realizing the nature of phenomena, you will not be able to guide others rightly on the path leading to the achievement of enlightenment. Now I will explain the six perfections in more detail.

Generosity

Generosity is an attitude of willingness to give away, without a touch of miserliness, your own possessions, body, virtues, and so forth. You give away your own possessions and wealth, and the virtues accumulated through giving these away should also be dedicated to others' benefit. The perfection of generosity is not dependent upon rooting out the poverty of all living beings; it is the ultimate development of a generous attitude. The texts speak of the importance of developing a sense of generosity, especially of giving your body to others. The physical body in itself is full of faults and defects, but with this body you can fulfill great aims by using it to help others instead of being possessive about it. The same applies to your possessions. If you are possessive about your belongings, you will accumulate more nonvirtuous actions by being miserly. But if you give your possessions away to others, they will serve a purpose, while increasing your practice of generosity. The virtuous collections you accumulate by giving these to others should be dedicated toward their benefit.

It is said that if you undertake the practice of generosity in this way, giving away your possessions, body, and your virtuous collections, the merit that you accumulate will be vast. Therefore, you should not be possessive about your belongings, nor should you work to hoard more and more, because possessions will prove an obstacle to your practice of generosity. The Buddha gave away his possessions and belongings for the benefit of others and achieved the state of perfect enlightenment. Having realized the futility of being possessive about your belongings, you should try to increase your sense of generosity and put it into practice by giving your possessions to others. A person who realizes the futility of being possessive and gives away his or her belongings, out of a pure wish to help others, is called a bodhisattva. It is said that since you have dedicated your own body and possessions and virtuous collections for the benefit of others, when you do use them, you must do so with the attitude of borrowing them from others and doing so for others' benefit.

In the practice of generosity, a stable and firm aspiration to enlightenment should be your motive. Whatever you give should be beneficial to others. The prac-

tice of generosity should be undertaken for the benefit
of others and should be done in a very skillful way, that
is, with the understanding that ultimately there is no
self to give or to receive. The practice of generosity
should be dedicated to the benefit of others, but it
should also be endowed with what is called sublime purity, meaning that the other five perfections should also
be present. For instance, when you give the Dharma to
others, you should have the morality of abstaining from
falling into a selfish attitude, and also you should have
the patience to endure hardships during the practice of
the path. There are three types of generosity: the giving
of the Dharma, the giving of fearlessness or protection,
and the giving of material possessions.

The intention with which you should practice generosity is the wish to achieve enlightenment for the
sake of others. When you actually engage in giving,
your attitude toward the persons to whom you give
should not be one of pity. You should see them as a
source of great kindness, contributing to your progress
in the practice of the Dharma. Although you should
not discriminate, you must pay special attention to
those who are materially poor and those who are suffering greatly. In short, whenever you practice giving,
you should always look and speak of the good qualities
of others and never speak of their faults. Your attitude
should not be influenced by a wish for reward or fame
or the hope of receiving something in return. And after
having given something, you should never regret having parted with that possession. Try to increase the joy

in giving, and never back away from situations in which you might have to actually physically engage in giving something away.

To increase and develop your sense of generosity, you should begin by giving away small possessions. With practice, this will lead to your not having even the slightest sense of apprehension or reservation in giving away your own body. It is said that one's state of mind depends always on what one is familiar with. For example, when we learn a language, we start right from the beginning with the alphabet. Initially it seems very difficult. If at that point we were given a complex grammar, it would not be helpful. But if we begin with the alphabet in a skillful manner, eventually even the complexity of the grammar will seem very easy. In the same way, if we train ourselves in giving away our material possessions, then later even parting with our own bodies will seem quite natural.

You should not postpone giving something away or wait for the other person to do something good. You should not give one gift when you have promised to give another, and you should not refer to your own kindness when you give something to make the recipient indebted to you. When you do give something away, you should do so out of pleasure and joy, with a pleasing expression. You should practice generosity yourself and encourage others to do so, to help others to develop a sense of generosity as well. Anything that harms others in the short term and that brings about sufferings and unhappiness in the long term is not a suitable gift. Anything that brings happiness in both the short and long term is suitable to be given to others. When you practice giving the gift of teachings, you should first analyze the nature of the listener to determine whether he or she will benefit from the teaching that you are thinking of giving. Otherwise, instead of being helpful to that person it might end up being harmful, and your listener may lose faith in the Dharma. In addition, you should not make gifts to hunters that they might use to kill animals, nor should you teach them techniques to catch animals. In some cases, refusal proves more beneficial than the giving. The bodhisattva should be skillful in such situations.

If you find yourself incapable of parting with something, you should reflect upon the futility of material possessions and also realize the impermanence of your own life. Sooner or later you will have to part with these possessions, so instead of dying in the grip of miserliness it is better to be free of the miserliness and give away your possessions now. Think to yourself, "I have been undergoing the torments of suffering in the cycle of existence just because I have not developed familiarity with the attitude of giving away my possessions. From now on I must change my attitude and develop a sense of generosity." To do this, mentally create all sorts of marvelous possessions and imagine giving them to others.

Ethics

The second perfection is ethics. Ethics is a state of mind that abstains from engaging in any situation or event that would prove harmful to others. The perfection of ethics is accomplished when you have developed to the ultimate point the conviction not to harm others. Ethics here is broadly classified under ten headings, that is, abstaining from the ten nonvirtuous actions. Ethics is like a cool rain, which extinguishes the fire of attachment, hatred, and anger within you. The intention with which you should undertake the practice of ethics should be nonattachment, nonhatred, and also right view. The observance of pure ethics should be influenced by fear of the consequences you will have to face if you indulge in negative actions, whose negative consequences have already been explained. The pure observance of ethics is like a beautiful jewel that suits everyone, irrespective of height, weight, age, and nationality. Material ornaments may look beautiful on one person but not on another, whereas the ornament of ethics looks beautiful on all practitioners irrespective of their physical appearance.

With the pure observance of ethics you will naturally command respect within the human community. Under the influence of ethics you will treat human beings in a proper and virtuous way, and you will be protected from indulging in negative actions. In the sutras it is said that even the dust of the ground on which the person with pure ethics walks is an object of veneration; such is the great quality of ethics. Your intention in observing pure ethics should not be confined to protecting yourself from engaging in negative actions but should also set an example for others, so that they too can be protected from the harm of negative actions.

Patience

Patience is a state of mind that forbears in the face of harms inflicted by others. There are three types of patience. The first is not being upset by harms inflicted by others; the second is voluntarily taking suffering upon oneself; and the third is being able to endure the sufferings involved in the practice of the Dharma. It is very important to reflect upon the great qualities and benefits of possessing patience. Those who have not undertaken any practice of patience will be seized at the time of death by a strong sense of remorse for the negative actions they have committed during their lifetimes, whereas those who have undertaken the practice of patience and endured harms inflicted by others will not have any sense of remorse at death. The most effective antidote to the attitude of abandoning others is the practice of patience. Patience also protects the practitioner from the harm inflicted by anger. It is said that even an instant of anger directed toward a bodhisattva can destroy the entire collection of meritorious virtue you might have accumulated over one thousand eons. So patience protects you from being discouraged when others harm you, and it also protects you from situations when your anger would destroy the entire collection of your virtues. It is an ornament admired by others; it is the armor that protects you from your own anger and from any harm inflicted by others.

The immediate effect of losing your temper is that you lose your calm, your presence of mind. Those around you will not be happy, because anger creates a bad atmosphere around you. Anger and hatred destroy your power of judgment, and instead of repaying someone's kindness you end up miserably retaliating. Even though you might enjoy material comforts, if your mind is filled with a powerful anger and hatred, you will not enjoy even the slightest pleasure because you will be in constant emotional torment. Realizing this, put great effort into this practice of patience and try to get rid of anger.

When someone harms you, you should not lose your temper and retaliate, but realize that the other person does not have any control over his or her emotions. The person is not doing it willfully but under the influence of negative emotions. The primary cause of someone getting angry and inflicting harm upon you is that he or she is under the constant influence of the delusions. Instead of losing your temper, you should develop mercy and compassion. The very simple point is that if individuals had control over their emotions, they would not do you harm at all, because what they seek is happiness. They would not work for their own downfall by accumulating the negative karma that comes from harming others. Because they do not have control over their emotions, there is no point in losing your temper.

You should analyze whether the anger and hatred and harmful intention are intrinsic to human beings or not. If anger is the essential nature of human beings, as heat is the nature of fire, there is nothing one can do to overcome it, and there is no point in retaliating when harmed. If, on the other hand, anger is not the essential nature of living beings but is just an adventitious quality, then again there is no point in losing your temper and retaliating, because what actually inflicts the pain is the instrument the person used, like a stick or a club. We should lose our temper at these instruments instead of at the person, but in fact we do not. Just as we do not lose our temper at inanimate objects like clubs, we should try to calm down and not lose our tempers at all. Instead, try to probe for the deeper cause of the harm. You will find that it is your own karmic actions, negative actions you have committed in the past, that have caused the person to harm you. Therefore, if you are going to lose your temper and retaliate, you should do so toward your own delusions and negative actions. There is no point in losing your temper toward others. It is only our delusions that cause us to face such circumstances and sufferings.

If I lose my temper and retaliate in response to some small experience of suffering that I am not able to bear, I will accumulate negative actions that will have a far-reaching impact in the future. Instead, I should feel indebted to the person who has harmed me, because he or she has given me the opportunity to test my own patience. Instead of losing our temper and retaliating, we should feel thankful to the persons who harm us. When we are struck, the pain is equally the result of the injury and of our own body. Without the body, we would not experience physical suffering. Therefore, if we are going to be angry, we should also be angry with our own body.

The practice of patience is very important for overcoming resentment and jealousy of the success and happiness of others. We should rejoice that instead of our having to work for all others, some individuals are capable of working for their own well-being. When we see such success, we should be happy and rejoice. We must overcome the sense of pleasure we experience when we see the downfall of our enemies or rivals and should not feel resentful or depressed about our enemy's success. Our resentment not only harms that person but also causes us to accumulate more nonvirtuous actions, which will cause our own downfall in the future.

In normal life, we often have more suffering than happiness. It is very important to be able to view all these experiences of suffering in the context of furthering our practice of the Dharma. If we have developed patience, in the sense of voluntarily taking sufferings upon ourselves, even though we might not be able to take on others' suffering physically, we will not lose our power of judgment. Even in ordinary life two people may be suffering from the same illness, but due to their different attitudes and ways of looking at things, one person suffers more because he or she is not equipped with the right attitude to face the situation, whereas the other person can face the situation better and can avoid the additional mental anguish and torment. We should remember that if a situation cannot be changed, there is no point in worrying about it. If the situation can be changed, there is also no point in worrying; we should simply work to change it.

If we do not face suffering, we will not have the wish to achieve liberation from the cycle of existence. That is one positive aspect of suffering. Without suffering, how can you have the experience of renunciation? In this context it is important to reflect upon the fact that up to this point from beginningless time we have been undergoing this cycle of suffering and torment constantly, never giving up our selfish motives, trying to cling to our self-importance, working for our own selfish ends. Now, we should realize the importance of changing that attitude and trying to work for the benefit of others. If, in the process, we have to face suffering, we will be able to endure it without losing the power of judgment and without being depressed about such experiences. There is no experience that through constant familiarity does not become easy in the end. Enduring sufferings in the process of the path is something that we can get used to.

It is very important to be decisive and courageous and resilient in your determination. When heroes see their own blood in battle, instead of being discouraged and losing heart, they become more determined; it serves as an impetus to fight more fiercely. That is the type of attitude that bodhisattvas should adopt when they meet situations in which they have to undergo sufferings. We should endure the suffering of poor physical circumstances in the process of the practice. We should endure the discomforts caused by people insulting us or speaking against us. We must bear the suffering of our own illness and aging. These should not overwhelm us; we should be able to endure them. We should be prepared to undergo the hardships that are involved in the process of leading an ardent life in the practice of the Dharma, devoted to the ultimate welfare of all sentient beings. We should never lose the force of our effort and should carry on with our practice without ever being resentful of the situation. On this stable foundation of patience we can construct our future realization of the path.

Effort

The next perfection is effort. Effort is the state of mind that delights in virtuous actions. It serves as the foundation for practices by which we avoid falling into the lower realms of existence. It is said to be the forerunner of all virtuous actions. If you are endowed with effort, all your studies and practice will be successful, because you will have no sense of weariness or discouragement. It is said that if you are endowed with perfect effort, free from any sense of discouragement or inadequacy, there is no endeavor in which you will not succeed. If, on the other hand, you are seized by laziness, you will make no progress in wisdom or in any other practice. A lack of effort brings downfall, not only in this life, but in the long term as well.

Armorlike effort enables you to endure any form of suffering or hardship in the process of working for the benefit of others. It protects you from discouragement and depression when faced with hardships. Your armorlike effort should be such that if you were to take rebirth in hell for innumerable eons, just for the sake of fulfilling the wishes of one individual, you would be prepared to do so. In order to achieve the effort needed to accumulate virtue, you must first identify the obstacle to effort, laziness. There are three types of laziness: the laziness of indolence, which is the wish to postpone what you have to do; the laziness of inferiority, which is the sense of not being able to do something; and the laziness that is attachment to negative actions, or putting great exertion into nonvirtue. To overcome laziness, you must reflect upon the fact that the practice of the Dharma has favorable consequences. You must also see the harm and futility of just engaging in senseless gossip and so forth. Senseless gossip and being constantly distracted and attracted to the worldly way of life serve as the greatest stumbling blocks to progress in our practice. To overcome the sense of inferiority, you must reflect upon the fact that all the Buddhas of the past have achieved enlightenment through the faculty of effort. Originally they were not Buddhas but were ordinary beings, like ourselves. But because they made great effort in the practice of the Dharma, they have been able to achieve the final goal. In order to overcome our lack of confidence we must realize that in order to achieve Buddhahood we have to be prepared to make some sacrifice. If we find that we are not yet prepared to make such effort, to part from our possessions, then we should realize that sooner or later we will have to part from these possessions and even from our bodies. Instead of having to uncontrollably part from them at the time of death when it would serve no purpose at all, we should give them away. Through the force of our generosity, we can at least derive some kind of benefit from them. Just as when you fall sick you have to endure the sort of physical pains that doctors inflict upon you by giving you injections, so for the sake of overcoming the great suffering that is the plague of the cycle of existence, it is necessary to endure a certain amount of hardship and physical pain on the path to enlightenment.

We should not feel depressed or discouraged by the fact that in order to achieve enlightenment we have to accumulate vast merit and wisdom for innumerable eons. The purpose for which we are trying to achieve this enlightenment is the welfare of all sentient beings. The number of sentient beings is limitless, and their sufferings are infinite. The process of working to relieve all these infinite beings from their limitless sufferings is bound to be a long and hard process. We must be prepared to make some sacrifices in the process. A bodhisattva is a being who, due to his or her compassion, love, and mercy for all suffering sentient beings, does not have even the slightest sense of regret or depression when he or she has to face suffering and hardship. There has never been a case where someone has achieved something with a lack of confidence. On the other hand, if we develop the courage and exert the necessary effort, even things that might have previously seemed complicated and difficult will eventually turn out to be very simple and easy. When you venture into an undertaking, first of all it is very important to assess the situation, analyze it, and see whether you will be able to do it or not. If you find that it is beyond your present ability or capacity, instead of trying to plunge into it immediately, it is better to back off and wait rather than leaving it half done. But once you have decided to do it, it should not be left half done; you should carry it through to the end.

It is said that in order to succeed in the venture you have undertaken, it is important to have confidence. This confidence does not have any negative implications; it is a simple sort of courage. Your confidence must be such that you are prepared to do anything alone, without depending upon the contribution or help of others. You should think that all other sentient beings, because of the influence of delusions, do not have the capacity or ability to work for themselves. You should have the confidence to feel that you have seen the harm of the delusions, that you will not allow yourself to remain under the influence of delusions, that you have the ability and capacity to work for the benefit of others. You should be confident never to let yourself come under the sway of delusions but always face and combat them. If you back down, even the slightest harm can destroy you. When a snake is dying, even crows act like vultures.

You should also cultivate the power of joy. Whenever you engage in these practices, it is very important that they are always accompanied by the faculty of joy. Your attitude of joy and pleasure in your practice should be just like the pleasure that children take in their games. This faculty of taking joy or pleasure in the practice of the Dharma overcomes your being satisfied with minor achievements. At the same time, you should not neglect the power of relaxation. When you make an effort in your practice and you feel tired and exhausted, it is important to relax so that you will feel refreshed and recharged and ready to engage in practice again. Otherwise, physical exhaustion will cause depression. It is said that the faculty of effort should be like a river, sustained and continuous.

When you apply the faculty of effort, you should try not only to combat the opposing factors that you are trying to overcome, but also to protect yourself from committing other negative actions as well. For example, when you are concerned with overcoming ignorance and you make constant efforts to identify ignorance and combat it, you may totally neglect other types of delusions and end up accumulating other nonvirtuous actions, like attachment. When a warrior drops his sword, he immediately picks it up without hesitation. In the same way, when you apply the faculty of effort, you should constantly apply the faculty of mindfulness, so that you do not fall under the influence of other negative states of mind. Mindfulness should serve as the primary factor for protecting yourself from the other delusions in the process of making effort, because even the slightest negative actions can have grave consequences. When you are pierced by a small poisonous arrow, the wound might be very small, but the poison pervades your entire body and eventually kills you. All the negative states of mind have that kind of potential. Some might seem not to be very grave, but all these emotions have this kind of potential. Your vigilance should be like that of a person forced to carry a glass of milk on his or her head under the threat of death if a single drop is spilled. Naturally that person would be careful not to spill anything. Your vigilance in undertaking the practice of the Dharma should be equally scrupulous. Under the circumstances it is very important to regret the negative actions that you have committed in the past and to develop a strong resolve never to indulge in them again. This will serve as a constant reminder never to lose the faculty of mindfulness. Just as a feather is carried on the wind, your body and mind should be sustained by the effort and joy you take in the practice of the Dharma.

Concentration

Concentration is the mental state of focusing single-pointedly on a virtuous object. Our ordinary mental state is one of distraction. Our ordinary minds are too uncontrolled and weak to be able to understand the nature of reality. And it is essential to understand the nature of reality if we are going to liberate anyone, ourselves or others, from the sufferings of the cycle of birth and death. It is therefore necessary to develop the mind into a suitable tool for investigating reality, like a strong microscope. It is necessary to develop the mind into a suitable weapon to sever the root of suffering, like a sharp sword. Concentration is the practice whereby one's ordinary, distracted, uncontrolled mind is developed to the point that it can remain powerfully, effortlessly, and one-pointedly on whatever object one chooses. Bodhichitta should be at the basis of the practice of concentration.

Tsong-kha-pa says that our minds have been under the influence of delusions since the beginning of time. The function of concentration is to gain control of your mind so that you can steer it to any virtuous object you choose. Up to now we have been under the influence of our minds, and our minds have been under the influence of delusions. Because of that, we have indulged in negative actions. As a result, we have to undergo unwanted sufferings. In order to terminate this vicious circle of the causes and conditions of suffering in the cycle of rebirth, we have to transform our minds and gain control over them. The mind, like a horse, should be directed to virtuous activities rather than to nonvirtuous ones. We should not let the mind simply wander into virtuous actions at random. In order to make your meditation effective, you have to do it in a systematic order with a degree of control. Otherwise, although you might initially experience a vivid visualization by accident, as long as it is not properly controlled, it is not very helpful. You will develop the bad habit of letting the mind go wherever it wishes. When you make real progress, on the other hand, you should be able to place your mind on a certain point easily and without difficulty. Until you reach that stage it is important to follow the proper sequence, just as you must lay proper foundations for a house if you are going to construct stable walls. You should have a plan right from the beginning, and you should decide in advance how much meditation you will do. During the main meditation itself you should be able to apply both mindfulness and introspection to see whether your mind is being distracted to other topics or not. It is said that at the beginning it is better to do shorter sessions, because if your session is very long there is a danger of coming under the influence of mental sinking or excitement. If you do a long session of two or three hours, even though you are spending the time, if your mind is not very attentive and comes under the influence of either mental sinking or excitement, your meditation will not be as effective as it should be. It is also important to have short sessions at the beginning so that when you do the meditations you will take pleasure in them. Otherwise, if you do a long session and do not enjoy it, there is a danger of becoming discouraged. When you see your meditation seat again, you will feel a sense of boredom or reluctance. However, if you do short sessions, when you resume your meditation you will actually enjoy doing it, because the impact of the earlier session will not have faded.

What is the role of sleep in practice? It is important not to sleep during the day or the first and last parts of the night. Westerners have a very strange habit. They go to bed very late at night and get up very late in the morning. If there is a special reason for doing this, that is another matter, but if not, it is better to go to bed early and get up early. Sleep is said to be a changeable mental factor. If you have a virtuous thought when you fall asleep, your entire sleep is said to be changed into virtuous thought. We have to go to bed for a specific amount of time, so try to cultivate a virtuous thought, like compassion, beforehand; then your entire sleep will be virtuous. Proper sleep actually sustains your body and maintains your physical health, which will help you in your spiritual practice. If you follow the Indian custom, you should wash your feet and then go to sleep. I doubt if many Tibetan masters followed this practice because of the cold. It is said that one should sleep like a lion, lying on the right side. Sleeping in this posture is said to have many advantages, for example that your body will not be overly relaxed; even though you fall asleep you will not lose the power of mindfulness; you will not fall into very deep sleep; and you will not have bad dreams.

When you go to bed, you should try to imagine a vision of light, so that you will not be subject to the darkness of ignorance during sleep. You should also have mindfulness and introspection and the wish to get up early. To be mindful before going to bed, just review the activities of the day or mentally go through your meditations. If you are successful in that, even when you are asleep you will not be out of control. Not only will your sleep be virtuous, it will also be possible to have virtuous thoughts. When you wake up, you will be mentally awake, but since the sense consciousnesses have still not regained their power, you can sometimes have a very clear state of mind. If you can use it for analytical practices, it is really very powerful. So you should have an intention to wake up at such-and-such a time, sleeping lightly, like animals do. By the force of that intention you will be able to get up as you plan. Tsong-kha-pa says that if you are able to use the activities of eating and sleeping properly, you can turn them in a virtuous direction and many negative actions will be prevented.

Tsong-kha-pa says that it is very important to realize that meditation is of two types, stabilizing and analytical, and that of these the skillful application of the analytic faculty of the mind is very important. For example, in order to make their silver and gold workable, goldsmiths and silversmiths first heat it and wash it and clean it and do all sorts of things so they can use it to make jewelry of any shape. Similarly, in order to overcome the root and secondary delusions, it is important first to reflect upon the faults and destructive nature of delusions and how they induce negative action—how as a result of this action one rotates in the cycle of rebirth. All of these have to be understood by applying the analytical faculty of wisdom, and only then can we hope to achieve the commitment to engage in the practice of the path. All of these analytical processes are like preliminaries that prepare the mind to benefit from the main thrust of the meditation. After having laid the proper foundation and made your mind fertile by such analytical processes, you can do any meditation, whether it concerns quiescence or insight.

When we do meditations, we should have an aim; we should make an effort. That effort is developed by seeing a purpose, and the purpose of our meditation should be understood. The better your understanding of the purpose, the more committed you will be in your practice. Tsong-kha-pa says that whether or not all the scriptures appear to be personal advice depends very much upon whether or not you can see how indispensable and important it is to practice both analytical and stabilizing meditation. He says that it is very sad that not only have people not studied properly, but even those who have undertaken a wide range of studies, when they actually engage in serious practice, discard all their studies and are satisfied with mere nonconceptuality alone. That is really very sad. If you do not try to explore the analytic faculty of the mind and just continuously remain absorbed in stabilizing meditation, simply maintaining nonconceptuality, you become less and less intelligent, and the wisdom to discriminate between right and wrong decreases. This is very dangerous.

Wisdom

Wisdom analyzes the nature of phenomena. There are many different types of wisdom, such as the five sciences: the inner science of religion and the four outer sciences of logic, medicine, grammar, and the arts. I speak here of the inner science. This form of wisdom is the foundation of all good qualities. Without the guidance of wisdom, all the other perfections, like generosity and ethics, would be like a group of people without a leader. The practice of the other perfections without the faculty of wisdom will not lead to the desired destination, toward the achievement of enlightenment. Compared to other faculties, like faith, mindfulness, effort, and so forth, wisdom is said to be more important because it is only through the force of wisdom, when complemented by the other faculties, that one can actually combat the force of the delusions. The other perfections, like generosity and ethics, depend heavily upon the realization of wisdom.

The power of wisdom is like that of a powerful king. If he is assisted by very skillful and intelligent ministers, he will not make any mistakes. In the same way, seemingly contradictory situations, like having very strong love and compassion and still not being polluted by attachment and desire, are due to the impact of wisdom. With wisdom, although you develop strong compassion and love toward others, you will never have desire and attachment toward them. If you are endowed with the faculty of wisdom, you will not fall to an extreme philosophical position of permanence or nihilism.

The obstacle to wisdom is ignorance, and the cause that promotes and increases ignorance is constant indulgence in pointless activities, such as laziness and sleeping too much. Ignorance also arises from having no joy or pleasure in the power of wisdom. The method for overcoming this ignorance is to increase your knowledge through study. For those who take serious interest in the practice of the Dharma, it is important to realize that the wisdom discriminating the nature of phenomena is the primary cause for achieving enlightenment. If someone is only concerned with teaching and not practicing, there is no need to acquire a broad knowledge; but instead of teaching it would be more beneficial if people like that kept quiet. For a serious practitioner, both learning and contemplation are very important. The progress you make in your practice should match the increase in your knowledge of the Dharma. Having obtained this precious human life endowed with a complex brain, we must make use of its special qualities and apply the unique faculty that we are endowed with, that is, the power to discriminate between right and wrong. This is done by increasing our understanding. The more you increase your knowledge, the better your understanding will be.

When you work for the achievement of wisdom, it is very important never to isolate your practice of wisdom from the other perfections. A practitioner who is working for the achievement of enlightenment actually requires realization of all six perfections. We can draw inspiration from the Buddha's own example. He first underwent severe penances and endured great hardships in the process of the path. Finally, under the Bodhi tree, he became enlightened and taught others what he had realized himself. Although it is initially very difficult for us to plunge into the practice of the six perfections, it is important at first to develop admiration for them and increase our understanding of them. This will eventually lead us to the true practice, enabling us to find freedom from the difficulties of the cycle of existence and enjoy the bliss of perfect enlightenment.

of the Buddha's teachings in Tibet and relates stories from various teachers throughout history. He also offers elegant, straightforward reflections on death, rebirth, karma, the Four Noble Truths, and the cultivation of the bodhisattva ideal and deeds: generosity, ethics, patience, effort, concentration, and wisdom.

HIS HOLINESS THE DALAI LAMA won the Nobel Peace prize in 1989 and is the author of two memoirs and several books on Buddhism.

Editor DONALD S. LOPEZ is Professor of Buddhist and Tibetan Studies at the University of Michigan.

JOHN F. AVEDON, General Series Editor of the Library of Tibet, is the author of *In Exile from the Land of Snows*, the definitive history of modern Tibet.